PARENTING UNDER FIRE

Parenting Under Fire

How to Communicate with Your Hurt, Angry,

Rejecting, Distant Child

Amy J. L. Baker, PhD

and

Paul R. Fine, LCSW

ROWMAN & LITTLEFIELD

Lanham • Boulder • New York • London

Published by Rowman & Littlefield
An imprint of The Rowman & Littlefield Publishing Group, Inc.
4501 Forbes Boulevard, Suite 200, Lanham, Maryland 20706
www.rowman.com

86-90 Paul Street, London EC2A 4NE

British Library Cataloguing in Publication Information available

Library of Congress Cataloging-in-Publication Data
Names: Baker, Amy J. L., author. | Fine, Paul R., 1955– author.
Title: Parenting under fire : how to communicate with your hurt, angry,
    rejecting, distant child / Amy J.L. Baker, PhD and Paul R. Fine, LCSW.
Description: Lanham : Rowman & Littlefield, [2023] | Includes
    bibliographical references and index.
Identifiers: LCCN 2023002558 (print) | LCCN 2023002559 (ebook) | ISBN
    9781538179062 (cloth) | ISBN 9781538179079 (epub)
Subjects: LCSH: Parent and child. | Interpersonal relations. |
    Interpersonal communication. | Parental alienation syndrome. |
    Alienation (Social psychology)
Classification: LCC HQ755.85 .B33468 2023 (print) | LCC HQ755.85 (ebook)
    | DDC 649/.1—dc23/eng/20230206
LC record available at https://lccn.loc.gov/2023002558
LC ebook record available at https://lccn.loc.gov/2023002559

We dedicate this book to Zoë An, with oceans of boundless love.

Contents

Contents

Introduction

If you are reading this book, it is probably because you're feeling that you are parenting "under fire," that your relationship with your child has become difficult. If your child is hurt, angry, rejecting, and distant with you, parenting is probably extremely challenging. We extend our sympathy to you and our wish that you find this book helpful in your efforts to retain or repair your relationship with your hurt, angry, rejecting, distant child.

This book is a natural extension of our previous efforts and builds on our work over the years with parents and children. Amy provides telephone coaching for parents who are concerned that the other parent of their child is trying to turn their child against them. She has conducted both qualitative and quantitative research on this topic, trained legal and mental health professionals around the world, and served as an expert witness in courts across North America. Paul has been providing individual, couples, and family therapy to clients affected by family discord and conflict for over four decades. Together, we have written three books on related topics and have worked together again to write this book, bringing our research and clinical experience to continue to try to help parents and their children. To put this book into context, it builds specifically on the ideas presented in our earlier work, such as *Co-Parenting with a Toxic Ex* (Baker & Fine, 2014a), *Surviving Parental Alienation* (Baker & Fine, 2014b), and *Restoring Family Connections* (Baker et al., 2020). In the first book, the focus is on parenting and co-parenting a child when one parent is turning the child against the other parent. That book is organized around how to respond to specific provocations of the other parent and is written for parents who still have ongoing contact with their child. The second book presents and analyzes a set of narratives about being cut off from a parent from the perspective of the parent of an adult alienated child, and the third book presents a series of activities that a parent and their adult formerly alienated child can engage in to repair the relationship. The current book takes a much broader perspective in aiming to help parents whose children are hurt, angry, rejecting, and distant regardless of the reason. The current book also presents theoretical frameworks and specific suggestions for parents of hurt, angry, rejecting, distant children of all ages and all stages of connection, including children who have totally cut off the parent.

This book is organized into three main sections. In Part I, theoretical and practical information is provided to parents with hurt, angry, rejecting, distant children of all ages (excluding infants) as long as there is some ongoing parenting time. The focus is on protecting the existing attachment between parent and child and developing strategies to respond to and reduce parent–child conflict. The four specific aspects of communicating with a hurt, angry, rejecting, distant child that are presented in this part of the book are enhance the attachment, don't take the bait, foster four values, and be a positive parent. This information is relevant for children of any age, as long as you have some contact with them.

In Part II, the focus is on how and why to send text messages to a hurt, angry, rejecting, distant child, especially one who is not engaging or engaging only minimally in parenting time. Topics include how and why to text with a hurt, angry, rejecting, distant child; basic messaging techniques; messaging tips and considerations; thirty types of text messages with 370 examples; and responding to the child's responses. This portion of the book is relevant for parents with children old enough to have a phone that can receive messages.

In Part III, the focus is on how to communicate by letter with a hurt, angry, rejecting, distant child. The philosophy of the letter is explained, homework is assigned, the components of the letter are explained with examples, and possible responses from the child are offered along with suggested responses from the parent. This section is most relevant for children who are at least older teens but could also be relevant for children of any age after that.

As the reader, you know best how to use this resource, and there is certainly no need to read all three parts of the book if one is clearly not relevant for you. However, there might be parenting strategies that you did not even know you could use, so you may want to dip into each section before you decide for sure whether it could be useful. Sprinkled throughout the book are reflections offered as opportunities for you to pause and think about how the content might apply to you or to have you check in with yourself to make sure that you are not flooded with negative emotions and if you are, to promote self-care. Please pace yourself and feel free to set the book aside as the need arises.

We welcome you to this book and share our most sincere wish that you find the information and activities helpful in your parenting journey.

Please note that we use the plural pronouns "they" and "them" to refer to a singular child, as opposed to "he" or "she" or "s/he," to avoid gender bias.

PART I

How to Communicate in Person with a Hurt, Angry, Rejecting, Distant Child

THE FIRST PART OF THE BOOK IS WRITTEN FOR PARENTS WHO have ongoing contact and communication with a child, yet they feel as if they are at least sometimes parenting "under fire." Your child may be hurt, angry, rejecting, and distant (HARD) for a variety of reasons, including oppositional defiant disorder, emotional disturbance, or reaction to trauma, or because the child is caught in a loyalty conflict and is receiving messages that you do not really love them. Whatever the reason, as a parent your job is to do everything you can to foster, nurture, and maintain a secure attachment with your child, reduce opportunities for conflict, and manage discord when it arises. Part I offers four overarching objectives for how to accomplish this: (1) enhance the attachment, (2) don't take the bait, (3) foster four values, and (4) be a positive parent. This information is relevant for parents of children of any age as long as you have some contact with them.

CHAPTER ONE

Enhance the Attachment

THE FIRST OBJECTIVE IS TO DO EVERYTHING YOU CAN TO enhance the attachment with your child. Many children who are hurt, angry, rejecting, and distant (HARD) behave that way because they have come to believe that you—their parent—are unsafe, unloving, or unavailable. This belief could come from inside the child (e.g., a child who has emotional problems and distorts reality) or outside the child (e.g., in a conflicted marriage or divorce when one parent tries to turn the child against the other parent). The belief could be false (the child has been lied to about you) or true (you have really engaged in behaviors that have caused your child to experience you that way). Regardless of the origin of the child's belief, it is essential as the parent of a hurt, angry, rejecting, distant child that you always behave in a safe, loving, and available manner with them. That does not mean, however, that you always agree with your child or that you always give them what they want. It means that you are always coming from a place of love and respect for your child. The more that your child experiences you as safe, loving, and available, the less likely it is that they will be hurt, angry, rejecting, and distant. There are eight specific strategies for enhancing the attachment: (1) be safe, loving, and available; (2) give lots of love and positive attention to your child every day; (3) turn "blah" moments into "ah" moments;

(4) speak your child's love language; (5) give your child show-you-care packages; (6) avoid badmouthing your child and others; (7) spend DEAR time; and (8) invite criticism.

BE SAFE, LOVING, AND AVAILABLE

One key way to enhance the attachment is to ensure that all of your interactions with your child are loving. And what we mean by that is that your interactions are not so much about *what* you do as a parent but *how* you do it that creates in the child a feeling that you are safe, loving, and available. For example, if your toddler says to you "I want ice cream for breakfast," you could say "That's ridiculous! Who eats ice cream for breakfast?" or "Who told you to ask me for ice cream for breakfast? Did your other parent put you up to this? You know that's not what we do." Now, you could talk that way to your child, and of course, it would be appropriate to set that limit and not let your child eat ice cream for breakfast. But *how* you say no affects the child's experience of the attachment relationship. You could say "That's ridiculous! Who put you up to this? Why would you think that?" But if you talk to your child that way, you are conveying that they are stupid, wrong, or bad or that they have been manipulated. And nobody likes that. When you talk to your child in a way that makes them feel bad about themselves, you create more hurt feelings. We believe that children should be free to express all of their wishes whether they be for ice cream, a new puppy, or a trip to the moon. They don't always understand the ramifications of what they are wishing for, so it would not be kind or appropriate to make them feel bad for expressing the wish. So instead, we recommend saying something like this: "Oh, don't you wish ice cream were a healthy breakfast choice! You can have ice cream later, and now you can choose between pancakes and waffles." You are *joining the child in the wish*. You're not humiliating them for asking for ice cream for breakfast, and at the same time, you're setting an appropriate limit. You're not getting out the bowl and ice cream scooper and dishing up rocky road for breakfast, but you're saying no in a loving and nonshaming way.

Now, as an opposite example, imagine that you want to give your teenager one hundred dollars. You could crumple up the bill, throw it at your child, and say "Here, take your stupid money, all right?" or you could hand it to your child with love in your heart and say "You know, I've been saving this money, and I was thinking about the right time to give this to you. I really feel like today would be a good day, so here's one hundred dollars. I just want you to have it." In both scenarios, the child is getting one hundred dollars, but in one, the gift is tainted with a parent being unloving and in the other, the gift is enhanced by the parent being loving. These are two examples where *how* you say something matters as much as *what* you say. And as much as possible, you need to try to be loving in how you speak to your child . . . always.

As another example, imagine that your child suddenly remembers at bedtime that they need to bring a posterboard to school the next day and they need to go out now to pick it up since the store will be closed in the morning. As the parent, you decide whether you want to take your child to the store past their bedtime. Most likely, if this is the first time that this kind of thing has happened, you will do it. If you chose to take your child to the store past their bedtime when you really don't feel like doing it, please do it with love in your heart. Don't grumble about how inconvenient it is, don't roll your eyes, don't lecture your child about how frustrated you are that they did not remember this earlier, and don't call your child names such as absent-minded, forgetful, or something worse. If you do that, you would be spoiling the experience with negative emotions. If you grumble and complain, most likely that is what your child will remember. At the end of the trip to the store, you might be feeling like the most accommodating parent, but your child will remember the way you humiliated them or complained.

To be clear, if it were truly inconvenient for you, then it is important to think about what lesson you want your child to learn from this experience. It *is* appropriate to say something the next day such as "It was inconvenient for me to have to take you to the store last night. What can we do so that you remember these kinds of things?" and then you can brainstorm with your child some solutions. Maybe the two of you will decide to post a note on the fridge saying "Is there anything [child's name] needs to bring to school tomorrow?" or perhaps the two of you will decide that you will ask your child when they get home from school if there is anything that needs to be picked up. The solution will depend on the age of your child and how frequently these kinds of things happen.

Reflections

- *How would it feel to join your child's wish, even if they are wishing for something you don't agree with?*
- *What lessons would you like your child to learn when they ask for something that is inconvenient for you?*
- *How can you set aside your momentary frustration to be emotionally present for your child?*

GIVE LOTS OF LOVE AND POSITIVE ATTENTION TO YOUR CHILD EVERY DAY

Children have an innate need for parental warmth, affection, attention, and love every day, and if they do not receive enough spontaneously from you, they are likely to try to extract attention from you in ways that don't feel very pleasant for you. Your child might be whiny and demanding, acting more babyish than they are just to get you to take care of them, they may interrupt you constantly making it hard for you to get things done, or they may be surly and uncooperative. In general, children would rather have negative attention than no attention, so if your child feels that they are not getting their need for love, affection, acceptance, and attention met they will behave in an unpleasant way to try to focus your attention on them. It is much better for everyone if you make sure that every day you are giving your child enough positive attention. Depending on the age and stage of development of your child, this could involve holding and cuddling and making lots of eye contact; it could also involve playing games, nurturing your child when they don't feel well, helping with homework, and talking about their thoughts and feelings. To be clear, you don't need to pay attention to your child every moment of every day. Rest assured that when children feel loved, they are usually happy to turn their attention to playing with toys, spending time with friends, and doing their own thing.

Another aspect of this to bear in mind is that most of your interactions with your child should be positive. The magic ratio, a term attributed to John Gottman in reference to marital relationships, can also apply to parent–child interactions. In essence, children benefit from receiving five positive statements for every negative statement. The easiest way to achieve this is to make sure that you spontaneously express positive affirmation to your child every day. You can start first thing in the morning with a loving greeting, and you can make spontaneous positive comments throughout the day. The comments are most effective if they are believable because they are reality based as opposed to hollow, overblown statements. Make sure to focus on your child's character as opposed to appearance, although periodic comments about their appearance are fine such as "That shirt looks awesome" or "Your haircut is really flattering." You can think of these spontaneous positive comments as filling your child's bucket (see below), and they fit nicely with the idea explored next of turning a "blah" moment into an "ah" moment.

TURN "BLAH" MOMENTS INTO "AH" MOMENTS

Another way to enhance the attachment involves taking what can be thought of as a "blah" moment and turning it into an "ah" moment. You can think of a blah moment as just sitting eating breakfast or sitting on the couch watching a movie—something that doesn't feel like anything special in that moment. You're just in the same place at the same time as your child.

And if you left it at that, later the child might be inclined to think that they're really not in much of an emotional connection with you. And if you are in a conflicted divorce, the other parent might say to the child, "Oh, you don't really have fun with that other parent. You don't really feel close and connected. You don't really have much of a relationship," and it will be easy for your child to go along with that idea because the memory traces of the time with you are sort of thin. You can think of it as a fragile thread. The memory trace of a blah moment is easily erased, blown away, and evaporated.

The goal then is to try to elevate that moment into an ah moment, which you can think about as "wrapping the thread" and strengthening that memory trace so that if the other parent or moment of self-doubt leads the child to believe that they really don't have fun with you and don't enjoy your company or don't have special moments with you, it will be a little harder for that false idea to take hold within the child. This is because with your added thoughtfulness instead of having a thin thread of a memory of the time with you, it will feel like a sturdier memory.

There are several ways to wrap the thread to strengthen the experience and hence the memory of your time together with your child. The first is through touch. If you are just hanging out on the couch, make sure to tousle your kid's hair, give them a shoulder squeeze, rub their feet if they like that, or whatever you can do to add that extra layer of warmth and connection with your child. Skin-to-skin touch can really enhance the feeling of closeness and connection. Affection is deeply rooted in our being, and touching settles the central nervous system and creates a feeling of calm and well-being. That is one way that you can elevate a moment.

The second way is through eye contact. If you're just sitting there having breakfast with your child, make sure to make eye contact with them. Don't get buried in your phone or reading the newspaper. Sure, it's fine to do those things sometimes, but make sure that you are paying attention and that you are emotionally available to your child. And you can do that through having a loving facial expression matched with eye contact. Eye contact increases the intensity of a moment, so it elevates that moment to feel more special.

And the third way is through verbalizations. You can say to your child "I just love being with you" or "I am so proud of who you are; you're such an awesome kid." You do have to mean it, though. It should come from your heart as opposed to being empty praise or generic and extravagant statements such as "You're the most wonderful person in the whole world" because that's not going to be believable for the child. It's about speaking from your heart.

Those are three ways to elevate a blah moment into a more meaningful feeling of connection between you and your child. You can touch your child, look at your child with a loving look, and make positive and loving verbalizations. All of those together can help increase the feeling of love and connection between you and your child. They can also help inoculate your child from becoming more hurt, angry, rejecting, and distant and/or prevent a mildly hurt, angry, rejecting child from becoming more so.

Reflections

- *What makes it hard for you to be emotionally present with your child as much as you would like or as much as your child needs?*

- *How does it feel when you have loving eye contact with your child?*

- *What are some genuine aspects or behaviors of your child that you can praise and appreciate?*

SPEAK YOUR CHILD'S LOVE LANGUAGE

Children vary with respect to their favorite ways to experience love by a parent. They may prefer intense and loving eye contact, a tender back rub and other forms of soothing touch, thoughtful gifts that show you really know what brings them joy, or positive affirmations of their worth and value. Others still really appreciate acts of service (e.g., doing their laundry, making their bed, or helping them with a project). No one type is better than another, and many children enjoy and need all these types of affirmation (and more!). Many children clearly have preferences, and it would be helpful if you knew what your child's was. The concept of a "love language" was first offered by Chapman and Campbell (2016), and they even have a website where kids can take a quiz to show their parents what their preferences are. Inviting your child to take the quiz and then following up on their preferences could be useful as well as a lovely bonding moment for the two of you. Remember that if you do make the effort to learn their preferences, it is important that you act on them. For example, if your child really likes acts of service, the next time you perform one, leave a note for your child such as "Laundry service by Mom/Dad" with a heart and smiley face. In that way you are showing your child that you paid attention to their preferences, which is another language of love.

Reflections
- *What are your love languages? Are they the same or different from your child's?*
- *Is there anything about your child's love language that is challenging for you?*
- *How can you remind yourself to keep your child's preferences in mind?*

GIVE YOUR CHILD SHOW-YOU-CARE PACKAGES

Many parents of hurt, angry, rejecting, distant children share that when their child is with them (if the child is still coming to spend time with them), they primarily spend that parenting time in their room away from them. In fact, some of these kids who come to spend time go right upstairs to their room and pretty much spend the entire time there away from the parents. In extreme situations, the child spends the entire time in their room having brought, for example, their own water to drink and food to eat. If you have reason to believe that your child will be in their room for some, most, or even all their time with you, then it might make sense for you to show that you care by creating a care package and leaving it on the child's bed. Some people may object to this idea, wondering why they should indulge their child and give them gifts and basically reward them for their "bad" behavior. It is our belief that when children are behaving that way, they're depriving themselves of the love and companionship that you have to offer. Imagine how hard it must be to spend an entire weekend—if not longer—holed up in one room in the house. We believe that rather than being angry at your child for squirreling themselves away, we think you should feel compassion for your child who feels that they must deprive themselves of companionship. If this idea appeals to you, then we suggest that you put together some little gifts for your child and place them in a nice gift bag or in a box and leave it on the child's bed. It might include activities to keep them happily occupied while in their room. Depending on the age of your child, it could be a crossword puzzle book, a sticker book, Silly Putty, Play-Doh, a coloring book and crayons, a celebrity gossip magazine, or an art project such as a kit to make their own friendship bracelets. The care package should also include some sweets and protein or granola bars to snack on and of course, some water to drink. Imagine what it would feel like for your child to go into their room and rather than it being a depriving and lonely place, it felt like your love has joined them in that space. It is a beautiful and unexpected way to show your child that you care. If your child is inclined to like this sort of thing, you might also include a stuffed animal because it's very soothing, comforting, and reassuring and another way for you to show your child that you love them where they are at and you want to provide them with the nurturance that you can given the situation. Assuming you're comfortable with it, you also could toss in a couple of chocolate kisses unless your child is on a diet, has difficulties processing chocolate, or has too many cavities or other struggles with sweets. Then you don't want to put in chocolate, but otherwise, kisses are symbolic kisses so it's a nice little added touch. And you can add a card to the care package. What you want to do is find a lovely card where the picture on the front of the card is something that your child can really relate to. If they love sunsets, then get a picture of a sunset; if they love puppies, get a picture of a puppy; if they like silly humor, then you want to get a silly, humorous card. On the inside of the card, you should write a lovely opening such as "Dearest [your child's name]. Then you can say, "I love you so much," "My heart is filled with love for you," or "You are my precious child and I love you so." For the second sentence, you want to express your pride for your child. You can say, "I'm so proud of you," and then add something about the child's character that you want to affirm. It could be "You're so kind to your younger sister," "You're so conscientious the way you always take care of the kitten," or "You're such a conscientious student the way you always get your homework done on time." Choose something meaningful that you want to praise your child for. It should not be something superficial, such as they are beautiful, because they don't really have any control over that. The third sentence should acknowledge that you and the child are not in a good place. You could say something like "I know we're in a rough patch right now," "I know you're not that happy with me right now," or "I know you're upset with me right now." The fourth sentence should express a positive vision for the future like "I know that we will get through this," "I believe we will get to a better place," or "I'm thinking about a time when you're feeling better about our relationship" and then sign the card "All my love, Mom/Dad." When you put the card in the envelope, don't lick and seal the envelope because that may discourage the child from opening the envelope to read the card. You don't want them to have to put in any extra work. So just tuck the flap into the back of the envelope. That way they can open it and read it, but they don't have to let you know that they opened and read it. When you leave those things on the bed, don't say anything to the child if they come out of the room to go to the bathroom or to get a glass of water or whatever. You don't want to seem too eager or that you're looking for some kind of affirmation from them that you're so terrific that you got them this great care package.

A version of the care package is the in-the-car care package. If your parenting plan involves your picking up your child from the other parent's home (or a designated pickup location), these transition moments can be very challenging for everyone, especially the child. It may help ease the transition if you have a small gift on the car seat waiting for your child. Don't draw attention to it; simply let it be there. Even if the object is small, make sure that it is tailored for your child, to show them that you really know them and love them. It could be the latest issue of a magazine focused on a hobby, a magic trick, a deck of cards, the latest in a series of books, or a food treat. The object can be a focus of attention that is shared (because you bought the object for your child) but provides your child with an acceptable excuse for not relating to you in the early moments of the transition, which can feel very awkward for your child.

Reflections
- *What are some objects that would really bring joy to your child that you could include in a show-you-care package?*
- *What are some other ways that you can show your child how much you care for them?*

- *How would it feel to give your child a care package knowing that your child will most likely not show their appreciation for your effort?*

AVOID BADMOUTHING YOUR CHILD AND OTHERS

The above suggestions (i.e., be safe, loving, and available; turn blah moments into ah moments; speak your child's love language; and give your child show-you-care packages) are all things that you can actively do. There is also something important to *avoid* doing as part of your effort to enhance your attachment with your child: make sure that you do not make negative comments about the child and their loved ones (notably their other family and their romantic partners). A common experience for some parents with hurt, angry, rejecting, distant children is that the parent wants to share their worries, fears, concerns, and theory of what is happening in the family with friends and family members. It is natural to want to share these feelings with others. However, extreme care must be taken regarding with whom you share your feelings, especially feelings about perceived bad acts on the part of the other parent. Children can be highly sensitive to the idea that you are spreading lies and negativity about the other parent within their community (e.g., to the parents of their friends), and this could be seen as worse than whatever thing the other parent did (e.g., ending the marriage or having an affair). Even if you feel certain that you have the moral high ground, it often does not matter to children. What matters is if you are perceived as spreading negativity within their circle. So share with only those people you feel you can completely trust. For others, it may help to have some handy phrases to use if someone tries to engage you in a conversation that would likely result in your being tempted to discuss your perspective. You can say, "Oh, that's a long story; I don't want to bore you with it. How are you doing?" or "Our family is going through some changes. . . . What's new with you?" It may be helpful to remind yourself that you do not owe anyone else your private and personal perspective and that the momentary relief of having an empathic ear is not worth the potential long-term damage you could do to your relationship with your child.

Likewise, you need to be very careful about with whom you share your perspective regarding your child's behavior. You may have a theory that your child is being alienated, turned against you, brainwashed, and unduly influenced, but it is highly likely that your child would be deeply offended and insulted if they knew that is what you thought. One way of understanding this is that most people do not even concede that advertising works, despite the fact that most, if not all, major corporations spend millions of dollars each year on both rationally and emotionally influencing the public to be interested in buying their products. Because humans like to believe that we operate rationally and with agency, directing our own choices, if your child knew that you thought their behavior was a product of undue influence, you would be offending their very sense of who they are.

Likewise, you might believe that your child has a serious emotional disturbance that is causing them to be so hurt, angry, rejecting, and distant, but it could be very painful, shaming, and embarrassing for your child if you shared that belief with other people in your child's social circle. Be extremely mindful of what you say about your child to others because it is likely to get back to them and can reinforce the idea that you are unloving.

Reflections

- *Are you clear in your own mind about with whom you can and cannot share feelings and details about your situation?*
- *If you need more support than you are getting from your personal network, would it be helpful to seek additional support from a professional, from a designated support group, or both?*

SPEND DEAR TIME

Sometimes children clamor for their parent's attention in a way that can be annoying. Many parents respond with irritation and a command or request for the child to give them some space, to stop pestering them, or to go occupy themselves somewhere else. This can increase the child's desire for closeness and connection because they feel that the parent is rejecting them. If your child is already feeling hurt, angry, rejecting, and distant, you don't want to exacerbate their feelings of being hurt by you. Instead of being annoyed with your child and trying to create distance from them, stop what you are doing, sit down wherever you are (within reason), and invite your child to have a hug or snuggle or whatever form of connection they need. You can think about this as DEAR time, in that you are dropping everything and replenishing your child. You can even use the term "DEAR time" with your child and ask them—if you sense that they need an extra dose of love and attention—"Do you want some DEAR time right now?" You might also consider creating a "cuddle corner" or some other named location in your home that is a designated place for you and them to go to get some extra doses of love and affection. Older children will probably find "cuddle corner" patronizing, so you will need to come up with a name that works for your child given their age, stage of development, and personality.

You may worry that if you "reward" your child's annoying behavior with a cuddle and extra attention that they will continue to be annoying. But the truth is that kids generally want to be busy playing games, spending time with their friends, and pursuing their interests; if they feel loved and satisfied, they will most likely move on to the next thing. Similarly, if we are thirsty for water and we take a drink, that does not necessarily make us want to drink more. Once that need has been satisfied, we stop drinking and move on. You want your child to have that feeling of fullness from your love so that they don't need to pester you to get it. If you are conscious every day of giving your child doses of love, affection, acceptance, warmth, and attention, your child will be much less likely to pester you for attention.

You may want to reference the book *Have You Filled a Bucket Today?* (McCloud & Messing, 2015), in which children learn that they have a sense of satisfaction when their "bucket" is filled and that they can fill their bucket by getting their needs met but also by doing nice things for others. If your child seems especially needy, you could ask them if their bucket needs a little bit of filling and what would help them do that.

INVITE CRITICISM

Rather than waiting for your child to be upset and then hoping that your child shares what is on their mind, you can try to identify and defuse situations and grievances as they arise. One way to do that is to be proactive and invite your child to share complaints with you on a regular basis. It is not likely that your child will make up a grievance just to have something to say, so you don't have to worry that you are making the relationship worse by doing this.

One way to invite criticism is to have a suggestion box in your home. You can periodically gather together, open the box, and read all of the suggestions together. This doesn't mean that you must honor every suggestion, only that you process the suggestions in a loving and respectful way. If your child "suggests" that there be no chores, you can have a discussion about what would happen if nothing got cleaned, and/or you can have a more serious discussion about how they feel about chores. You can explore whether your child feels that chores are unfairly distributed or too onerous. You can discuss ways to make the chores feel more palatable for your child. Likewise, if your child "suggests" that you eat fast food every day for dinner, you can explore the nutritional elements and cost of these foods. For example, you can explore what the family would have to give up to afford eating out more often. Perhaps you could also discuss your child's suggestions for improving home-cooked meals.

Another way to invite criticism is simply to say to your child, "Hey, honey, I hope that I never hurt, frustrate, or disappoint you, but if I have, I hope that you will let me know. Anything you would like to share?" or "How am I doing? What could I do better for you?" Again, you are not necessarily going to agree with your child about every complaint or suggestion, but you can certainly hear your child out. It will help create more open communication between the two of you and allow you to nip grievances in the bud rather than having them fester.

It is essential that you respond to the suggestions and criticisms with a loving and gracious attitude. If you become sullen, angry, resentful, bitter, defensive, or sarcastic, then you will be missing an opportunity to create a feeling of closeness with your child. And the lesson that you are trying to teach would be subverted by your mixed message. You want your child to experience a positive feeling from sharing their criticism in a safe environment. Similarly, it would be unfair to your child to invite them to criticize you and then emotionally punish them for doing so. Also, make sure to avoid any references to the other parent—or any other third party whom you might feel is influencing your child—by complaining that your child never seems to complain about that person. The bottom line is do not invite criticism unless you are in a place where you can hear it with an open mind and a caring heart.

Reflections

- *How does it feel to think about inviting your child to be critical of you?*

- *How can you be a role model of embracing and considering criticism without becoming defensive?*

- *Are you concerned that by encouraging criticism you are unleashing a storm of negativity from your child? Do you feel ready to respond to criticism in a loving way?*

In sum, enhancing the attachment between you and your child is the most essential component of your communication strategy. The feeling that the child has when they are with you—that you are safe, loving, and available—is *the* essential ingredient to maintaining and/or repairing the relationship. If your child does not feel that you are safe, loving, and available, then this is something to really focus on as an area of improvement. These three qualities/requirements should guide all that you do and all that you are when you are with your child.

Don't Take the Bait

Children who are hurt, angry, rejecting, and distant often behave very provocatively. They can be uncooperative, negative, contemptuous, surly, and arrogant and can really push your buttons! But if you respond with anger or depression—normal human reactions when your child is hurt, angry, rejecting, and distant—you are possibly reinforcing in your child's mind the negative idea of who you are. The negative idea (i.e., that you're unsafe, unloving, and unavailable) is reinforced when your child behaves in a provocative way and you respond by screaming at or hitting the child or sobbing. The child can then say, "Gee, I guess it is true; this parent is a creep, a monster, or a loser. We don't have any fun together. All we do is fight." You do not want to inadvertently reinforce the negative idea. Imagine that your child accused you of beating them when they were a baby. Let's say you have never hit your child before, not even spanking, but your child is pushing your buttons and in your face with what you perceive to be difficult and unpleasant behavior and you react by spanking or even slapping. Well, now you've made the negative idea true.

To be clear, children—especially those who are hurt, angry, rejecting, and distant with one parent while not being that way with the other parent—hold their parents to very different standards. If your child is already hurt, angry, rejecting, and distant with you, then you will be held to a higher standard than the other parent. That is the reality. You cannot afford to take the bait. The other parent can engage in suboptimal and even egregious behavior. But if they are already the preferred parent, your child is going to prefer them pretty much no matter what, believe what they say, take their perspective, and see the world through their eyes no matter what their flaws. Your child will most likely cut that parent all kinds of slack. That parent can miss special events or be ungenerous or dishonest. They can be mean or lazy, but if they're the preferred parent, your child will minimize and/or deny their flaws, and they are not going to cut you any slack whatsoever. You don't have the luxury of taking the bait when your child behaves in a way that you find unpleasant. You need to learn what to do when your child is pushing your buttons. This chapter will present six strategies: (1) learn how to regulate your emotions, (2) avoid negative labels, (3) respond respectfully to unpleasant behavior, (4) use the five steps for false accusations, (5) use the modified five steps for true accusations, and (6) avoid false allegations of child abuse or neglect.

LEARN HOW TO REGULATE YOUR EMOTIONS

In your efforts to not take the bait, it is essential that you learn how to regulate your emotions, especially negative emotions of sadness, anger, fear, worry, disgust, or resentment. It is quite common for parents whose children are rejecting them to feel very emotionally aroused. For example, if your child calls you by your first name, tells you that their stepparent is more of a parent than you will ever be, spies on you, keeps secrets from you, speaks to you in a demeaning tone, or uses words and phrases from the other parent that are triggering for you, you will understandably experience negative emotions. However, if you become emotionally overaroused with sadness, anger, or fear, it is hard if not impossible to be emotionally available to your child.

As an example of taking the bait, one father shared that one day his seven-year-old daughter came for her parenting time with him and excitedly told him that she and her mommy had bought a calendar. The father enthusiastically responded, "How lovely, a calendar! Tell me about it." Well, the daughter said, she and her mommy had decorated all of the days on the calendar that they would be together with stickers of cupcakes and rainbows and unicorns. The father again enthusiastically responded, "Cupcakes and rainbows and unicorns! How lovely. I know how much you like them." He then asked, "What about the daddy days? How did you decorate them?" The daughter explained that those days were colored black. The father shared that upon hearing that the daddy days were colored black, he went into an emotional tailspin and became sad and dark. He sadly admitted that he was emotionally unavailable to his daughter because he was so flooded with negative emotions on hearing how the other parent had blackened the days on the calendar, signaling to the daughter that she would not have fun when she was with her dad. In effect, he took the bait and allowed the other parent's provocations to influence his relationship with his daughter. She most likely did not realize that the father was being manipulated; she just knew that her time with him was not so fun, just as her mommy had suggested. As another example, if your child accuses you of not loving them and you respond with anger and frustration, demanding that your child justify such a crazy idea, you are essentially reinforcing the very idea that you are trying to counter.

Controlling your emotions is the first step to not taking the bait. Thankfully, there are things you can do to ensure that you do not react based on negative emotions. First, you can always say to your child, "Let's deal with this later." For example, you might ask your child to put their cell phone down, and they do not do what you ask and perhaps speak to you in a demeaning tone of voice, claiming that their phone was a present from the other parent and is a lifeline to that parent and they do not have to give it to you.

In response, you are likely to feel triggered and upset. Please bear in mind that there is no rule that dictates that you must address the situation in the moment. Children are not puppies; they do not need to be scolded or disciplined immediately after an incident. It is acceptable to say to your child, "Boy, I'm not happy that you're not putting your phone down; we're going deal with this later." This is by far a better strategy than letting your emotions get the best of you because you may make a regrettable mistake. For example, if you grab the cell phone out of your child's hands, you might scratch your child, or your child might fall and bump their head, both of which could actually cause you to end up with a physical abuse investigation on your hands. Here, the bottom line is never to touch your child in anger, because your child could accidently get hurt, which could cause your child to be afraid of you. Once the anger takes over, you may not actually realize how hard you are touching your child, and you can cause fear and pain in them, which is obviously the opposite of being safe, loving, and available.

Second, you can even say "Let's deal with this later" to yourself and schedule a time to process something that is going on so that it does not take you out of the moment with your child. It often happens that a parent is having a calm and maybe even loving moment with their child and they notice that the mail was just delivered, including an envelope clearly from the attorney, possibly bringing some upsetting news. You might receive a notification on your phone that your ex posted a message on a parent communication app, or perhaps you receive an email from your ex. It is recommended that you not direct your attention away from your child but rather say to yourself "I can deal with this later." Try not to let bad news interrupt your precious moments with your child. Most likely, if you check the mail, text, or email, you will find that your mind and energy have been diverted away from your child. This could inadvertently reinforce the idea that you are not available to them.

Third, remember to engage in encouraging positive self-talk. Self-talk is what we say to ourselves inside our head and can be negative or positive. Negative self-talk can magnify a bad feeling. For example, if you say to yourself "This is the worst thing that has ever happened to me" or "I just can't take this anymore," it will probably make you feel worse. What you say to yourself inside your head affects your mood, energy, and feelings of hopefulness or despair, which in turn can affect your behavior. Try to be aware of how you engage in self-talk. Notice if you are using negative self-talk, and try to steer yourself toward a more positive direction. That does not mean that you say false things to yourself such as "Oh, I love being taken to court by my ex" or "It is so charming when my children reject me." It does mean that you try to interrupt the negative and replace it with something that is more hopeful while still being true. You could think "This is really tough right now" or "I wish that things were going better for me." Try to avoid catastrophizing such as "This is the worst thing that has ever happened" or "I can't handle this." Try to remind yourself that you are strong, capable, and resourceful and that you can and will deal with whatever comes your way. You want your positive self-talk to be encouraging and hopeful, not falsely positive and unrealistic.

Four, engage in activities that can release tension from your mind and body. When you are holding a lot of tension, it is hard to feel calm and centered, and it becomes hard to avoid taking the bait. There are many tools and techniques for calming down and releasing tension. There are apps on smartphones to help guide you to be calmer if you want a structured approach, or you can simply take deep breaths using the box technique (i.e., breathe in slowly counting to four, hold your breath for four seconds, slowly release the air through your mouth for four seconds, and repeat five times). Deep breathing is an effective method for calming the central nervous system, which helps you stay calm and emotionally regulated. Another easy action is to plant your feet on the floor because that signals to your body that you are safe (i.e., you are not on your tiptoes preparing to flee danger).

And finally, if you feel that a situation is not going well with your child, remove yourself from the situation. You can go to the bathroom and splash some cold water on your face and give yourself a pep talk. It is a safe space to which you can go to interrupt a negative interaction and prevent you from doing or saying something that you will regret.

Reflections
- *What are some times in your life when you had to call on your inner strength and manage your emotions?*
- *What are some positive things you can say to yourself to remind yourself that you are capable and resourceful and can handle whatever comes your way?*
- *What are some of your favorite strategies for keeping yourself calm when you are feeling stressed?*

AVOID NEGATIVE LABELS
Another aspect of not taking the bait is to avoid thinking or using pejorative labels when your child is behaving in an unpleasant manner. Many parents with angry, hurt, rejecting, and distant children share that their children behave in ways that are very unpleasant. They often use the words "rude" and "disrespectful" when describing their child. If your child behaves in such a way toward you, you might feel that it is your duty as a parent to provide the child with feedback about their problematic behavior. You probably do not want your child going through life thinking that it is okay to sneer at people, call them unkind names, or ignore them. Part of your job as a parent is to socialize your children so that they can be functioning members of society, so it is understandable that you feel that you need to respond when your child is being unpleasant with you.

At critical times like these we need to remember the importance of not using a negative label when talking with your child—

even when their behavior is unpleasant. It is not helpful to refer to somebody else as "toxic," "abusive," "nasty," "disrespectful," or "rude." It's generally demeaning, demoralizing, and humiliating for the child, and it doesn't help foster a feeling of closeness between parent and child. When a parent refers to the child with a negative label, they often come to identify with and embody the label rather than being motivated to change their behavior. They think "Well, if Mom/Dad already thinks I am a slob, I guess I might as well be a slob." The negative label reinforces the undesirable behavior, so in addition to being unkind, it is counterproductive.

One thing to bear in mind is that when your child is behaving in an unpleasant manner, it is often because they are feeling hurt. Most likely they are feeling that you don't really love and care for them, you want to harm them, and/or you cannot be bothered to pay attention to them. Try to remember that their unpleasant behavior is coming from an emotional wound that needs to be addressed before you can address the behavior that is problematic.

Reflections
- *What are some negative labels that come to mind when thinking about your child?*
- *How can you think about these attributes in a more loving and empathic manner?*
- *How can you remember to respond to your child's unpleasant behavior with loving kindness?*

RESPOND RESPECTFULLY TO UNPLEASANT BEHAVIOR
You might be wondering what you should do when your child is behaving in an unpleasant manner, whether they are sneering at you, yelling at you, cursing, or engaging in some other behavior that conveys a negative message to you about your worth and value. You are a human being, and you have a right to be respected,

to not have anyone treat you in a way that you find very unpleasant. But you cannot—in our opinion—start with negative feedback such as "How dare you talk to me that way" or "Go to your room and don't come out unless you can be pleasant." Those kinds of responses do not make sense because if your child is yelling or cursing at you or spitting or doing something else that you find very unpleasant, it is most likely because your child is upset with you. If you start with the negative feedback about their behavior, you are essentially going to be perceived as saying that you care more about your feelings than their feelings. You are in essence reinforcing the ideas that you do not really care about them. Therefore, ideally you will begin your response by acknowledging that your child is upset and that you care. This way you maintain your position or role as protector and caretaker of your child. Your empathic response is what creates a feeling of connection. You can address the unpleasant behavior afterward.

We recommend a three-part response. The first part is to acknowledge that the child is upset. You can begin by saying something like "Wow, you are really upset right now, and I want to understand what's going on." Second, you can explain in a non-pejorative fashion what the child is doing that is uncomfortable or unpleasant for you without any negative labels attached to the behavior. You might say something like "You're talking in a tone of voice that is very distracting to me," "Your voice is so loud that it is hurting my ears," "Your cursing at me really doesn't feel good to me," or "I really don't want to be spit at." You are describing something that is uncomfortable or unpleasant for you but not in a way that will make the child feel bad about themselves. What you want to do is provide neutral feedback such as "I don't want to be cursed at" or "I don't want to be yelled at." Then you end this strategy with an invitation to the child to tell you what's going on in a more pleasant way.

Here is what the whole response would sound like from start to finish using an example of the child yelling at you. You would say "Wow, you are really upset, and I want to understand what's going on. You are speaking really loudly, and the volume is bothering my ears. Could you please say it again in a quieter tone of voice?" This strategy is designed to help the child feel that you care about them, you are safe, you are loving, and you are available. This is what can help protect the relationship with the child when your child is coming at you with a lot of anger and hostility. You are providing them with corrective feedback about their problematic behavior in a way that prioritizes the relationship.

Reflections

- *What are some ways that your child's behavior is unpleasant for you?*

- *What do you think your child is feeling and thinking when they are behaving in an unpleasant manner?*

- *Would it help to practice these steps so that you can authentically implement them if the need arises?*

USE THE FIVE STEPS FOR FALSE ACCUSATIONS

One of the most challenging aspects of relating to a hurt, angry, rejecting, distant child is when the child accuses the parent of doing something that the parent feels is mostly if not entirely untrue. The problem for the parent is that the logical and rational response, which is to say some version of "that's not true," actually does not work, especially if the parent responds with "That's ridiculous; why would you believe that?" or "That's a lie; you know that's not true." While it seems logical to want to explain to your child that they are wrong for thinking you did this terrible thing that you did not do, that does not work. That is because if you say to your child "That's ridiculous," you are basically calling your child a fool or an idiot for believing something like that and therefore, you are insulting your child. If you tell your child that they know something isn't true or that something is a lie, then you are calling your child a liar. Since calling a child a liar or an idiot is hostile and unkind, it will only exacerbate the situation, so you want to avoid responses like that. Moreover, if you respond with hurtful responses like that you are probably reinforcing a negative idea of who you are.

Another reason these responses don't work is because it is possible your child does not really care about the thing they are complaining about anyway. On some level, of course, they care if they think you did something terrible, but really, the main thing they are feeling in the moment is that you don't love them. Your showing them that they are mistaken about the details does not address the underlying issue. Evidence for this point comes from the fact that many parents have tried to address the falsehood that the child is claiming and it made no difference. A parent whose child claimed that they stole the child's college money might, for example, race upstairs and locate the most recent bank statement showing that the money is safely in the bank. According to many parents who have responded this way, it makes absolutely no difference because the child's underlying feeling of being unloved by the parent is not addressed.

What could be helpful in this situation is something called the five steps, which are briefly described in Baker et al. (2020) but expanded upon here. Using the five steps as a texting strategy is explained in Chapter 9.

The first step is called gratitude, and this means telling your child that you are glad that they are sharing a complaint with you. We recognize that we do not actually feel happy when a child complains (especially about us). No one really thinks "Yippee, my child is complaining!" But it is important that you not just express gratitude but that you feel gratitude. So let's start with the premise that all children have grievances about their parents. All parents at some point hurt, frustrate, and disappoint their children, so the question you can ask yourself is "To whom do I want my child complaining about me? Do I want my child complaining to others when they think I've done something that hurt, bothered, or frustrated them, or do I want them to bring the complaint to me so that we can work through the problem together?" Therefore, if your child is complaining to you, you should be feeling grateful that at least your child is coming to you with the complaint and not complaining about you to someone else.

Likewise, another alternative that's not as good as your child coming to you with a complaint is your child shutting down. Many parents of a cutoff child have had the experience of the child basically saying "I'm done! I'm not talking to you" and shutting the parent out, going into their room for the whole visit, or putting on their earbuds and basically not paying any attention to the parent and not investing any energy in the relationship. For older cutoff children, the cut off could result in near or total lack of communication. If you are in that situation, most likely you are desperate to hear from your child what is on their mind. You might be pleading with them, saying "What is it? What have I done? What are you upset about?" So when your child complains to you, even though you don't necessarily enjoy it, you could feel gratitude that at least your child is talking to you and sharing the complaint with you.

A helpful analogy might be if your young child skins their knee at the playground and they run to you to kiss their bloody knee and make it better. Do you really want to kiss a bloody knee? Probably not. It's kind of gross, but it reinforces the bond between you and your child. And you wouldn't want your child bringing their bloody knee to somebody else, right? A complaint about you from the child is sort of like the bloody knee. The child is bringing something to you that is not particularly pleasant, but there is an implicit acknowledgment that there is a relationship and that is a good place to start.

Another way to think about this—just to continue with this idea about why you should feel gratitude—is if you have ever been single and you go out on a couple of dates and the person is more into you then you're into them and you don't want to have that next date. And the person is asking you "Why? How come?

What did I do? Please tell me." And you feel like, "Ugh, I can't be bothered. I don't want to invest any energy into explaining myself to this person." So you don't want to tell the person what they did that you didn't like because you know that by investing energy into this relationship and explaining what's bothering you, you are giving the person hope that if they just fix something, then you would want to be with them. But if you're truly done with the relationship, you are done. You don't want to fix anything, you don't want to move forward with that person, and you don't want to invest energy and explain what you didn't like. Of course, your kids should not be empowered to leave you—like a failed dating relationship—but unfortunately, you could be at the receiving end of just that. As long as your kids are bringing a complaint to you, they are telling you in so many words that they are not done and that they are still willing to invest energy into this relationship. And that's why you can and should feel grateful.

Here is how to express gratitude. If you are implementing the five steps in person (how to do it in text format is explained in Chapter 9), virtually, or on the phone, it is important to do so with positive feeling energy in your voice because that's part of you investing energy in the relationship. If you talk to your child in a blasé, nonchalant, or casual manner, you are conveying that you don't really care, and you definitely do not want to do that. You want to convey to your child that you are investing energy in the relationship because they matter to you. Step one should be about five sentences in length. It is not "Gee thanks" because that is too low key and too brief. It does not convey the full extent of your gratitude toward your child.

Here's how you express gratitude in about five sentences using as an example a child named Chris whose complaint is "You beat me when I was a baby," although this could work for any complaint that's mostly or entirely untrue. The complaint could be you stole their college money, you never paid attention to them, you were never close, you're a cheapskate, you don't listen to them, you don't cook food they like, or you yell all of the time. As long as the complaint is mostly untrue and you are tempted to respond with "Why would you say that? You know that is not true," then the five-step method is offered as an alternative.

The first sentence of the first step—called gratitude—is to say the child's name, say thank you, and repeat the child's complaint using the child's words. So if the complaint is "You beat me when I was a baby," you're *not* going to say "Thanks for telling me that ridiculous idea that your other parent brainwashed you into believing." And you're not going to say "Thank you for telling me that you think I'm the worst parent in the whole world ever" because that's not what the child said. You're going to repeat back the child's complaint using the child's words to show that you were listening, because listening is an act of love. But that's only one sentence, and the gratitude step is supposed to be five sentences. So here is how you expand gratitude into five sentences:

I cherish our relationship and hope that I never hurt, frustrate, or disappoint you, but I always want to know if you feel that I have. I am so grateful that you are letting me know what is on your mind. And you know what? It's easy to complain about someone behind their back. It takes courage to look me in the eye and tell me what is going on, and I am really proud of you today because I think you have been really brave.

So step one is loaded with positive words including *pride*, *cherish*, *appreciation*, *courage*, and *bravery*. You want your child to walk away from the experience feeling good about themselves. It might help to engage in a little thought experiment. Imagine that you have a boss and you say to your boss "Hey, boss, I'm kind of upset. I feel like you threw me under the bus at the staff meeting today." Now imagine if your boss said to you "What are you talking about? That's ridiculous!" and then imagine if instead your boss said to you "Thank you so much for telling me you think I threw you under the bus at the staff meeting this morning. I value you as an employee so much. I'm so glad that you're telling me that I did something or you think I did something that didn't feel good to you. You know it's easy to complain about me behind my back. You've got guts coming in here and telling me to my face. That's awesome." Imagine how you would feel under those two scenarios. I imagine the second response is how you would prefer to be spoken to and that you would feel better about yourself and your boss if the boss spoke to you with five sentences of high-intensity gratitude. And that is what you want for your child, to feel good about themselves when they are with you. That does not mean that you always agree with them or always give them what they want, but it means that you are always loving and respectful. Not only will they feel good about themselves, but they will feel good about you—and that is what you want.

The point is that you want to create a positive reinforcement for your child for complaining to you so that your child will do it again. If you make them feel ashamed or ridiculed or you respond with anger and hostility, your child may not want to bring the next complaint to you.

Step two is called compassion. This is also about five sentences of high-intensity speech. The purpose of compassion is to show your child that you are paying attention to their emotional state in the moment. When your child is telling you "You beat me when I was a baby," is the child saying it with anger, sadness, confusion, fear, or some other emotion? Someone who is feeling sad looks and sounds very different than someone who is afraid, and your job is to determine how your child is feeling in the moment.

To determine what your child is feeling as they are telling you what is bothering them, you are going to pay attention to four things: (1) the words your child is using (your child might actually say "I am furious with you" or "I am feeling really sad that you . . ."); (2) their tone of voice (someone who is sad sounds very different than someone who is angry); (3) their facial expression (this is the primary way that people communicate their feeling state. Someone who is sad has a very different facial expression than someone who is afraid); and (4) their body and posture (the energy and position of the body convey emotions). You're going to pay attention to those four things. Then you're going to take an educated guess as to what your child is feeling, and you're going to reflect that back to your child with four or five sentences of high-energy speech.

The truth is that this is very hard. When we are attacked, we want to defend ourselves, and we go into fight, flight, or freeze mode. We don't go into compassion mode. It is possible that the roots of this go all the way to our ancestors. Imagine a scenario of an ancestor back on the African plain when they were being chased by a lion. They weren't thinking "Oh, poor lion. What's he going to have for dinner tonight?" Those people who felt compassion while being attacked were probably distracted. They weren't as focused on escaping the lion, and they probably stumbled and got eaten by the lion. Those are not our direct ancestors. We are more closely descended from people who went into fight, flight, or freeze mode, and they saved themselves. They weren't thinking about the lion. They were focused on survival. They went into tunnel vision mode where all of their energy and resources were channeled into survival. There was no room for compassion. So it's in our DNA to feel defensive, instead of compassionate, when we are attacked.

Luckily, there's a couple of easy ways to override the shutdown of compassion while we're being attacked. The easiest thing is just to take a couple of deep breaths. That calms the central nervous system and gets you out of fight, flight, or freeze mode. You can also say to yourself "My child is not a lion. My child is not going to eat me. This is a suffering child. My child is hurt and upset." And those kinds of thoughts should allow you to pay attention to your child's words and tone of voice, facial expression, and body posture.

Here is how to express five sentences of compassion using the example of the child who thinks that you beat them when they were a baby and is very angry. You would say:

No wonder you are so angry! You think I beat you when you were a baby. And boy, can I see how angry you are feeling right now. I can tell from your tone of voice that you are feeling angry. You are speaking loudly and with a stern tone. I see the anger in your face. You have a scowling look on your face and your jaw is clenched. And I can see that you are holding tightness in your body. You are standing there with your hands on your hips. You look like you are ready to go to battle.

The purpose of this step is to show your child that you are paying attention to their emotional state in the moment.

If the child is sad, you might say something like this:

No wonder you are so sad! You think I beat you when you were a baby. And boy, can I see how sad you are feeling right now. I can tell from your tone of voice that you are feeling sad. You sound like your voice is cracking as if you were about to cry. I see the sadness in your face. You are frowning, and your eyes are filling up with tears. And I can see the sadness in your body. You are sitting there with your shoulders slumped, giving yourself a hug to help you feel better.

Again, the purpose of this step is to show your child that you are paying attention to their emotional state in the moment. Step three is called empathy. When done face-to-face or on the phone (as opposed to text messages), this is also about five sentences long and is spoken with energy. The purpose of step three—empathy—is to show your child that you are trying to look at the situation from their point of view. This is unrelated to whether you agree or disagree with your child. Using the same scenario as before, here is what it would sound like:

You know, Chris, if I were a seventeen-year-old girl and I thought my mom beat me when I was a baby, I would be steaming mad too.

So in the first sentence of step three, empathy, you are plugging in the specifics of the situation including the child's name, their age and gender, who you are to them (mom or dad), what their complaint is, and what you surmise them to be feeling. Then you continue by saying,

> *I am really trying to understand our relationship from your point of view. I'm trying to look at things from your perspective. If I believed what you believe, I would probably be feeling what you are feeling. I get where you are coming from.*

Step four is called the minor correction. This is your opportunity to correct the child's false narrative. It is important to note that this step is called the *minor* correction, and this is so for two reasons. The first is that it's minor (small) in terms of energy. Instead of being high energy like the first three steps, step four is low key, nonchalant, and casual. It's also called the minor correction because it's short. Step four should be one sentence. This is your chance to share with your child your perspective. There are different versions depending on the complaint.

If the complaint is 100 percent objectively false, such as you stole my college money and the money is still in the bank, then you could say "That didn't actually happen." Just like that, very relaxed. You're not saying "That. Did. Not. Happen." But most of the time the accusation is subjective, so it wouldn't be appropriate to say "That didn't happen." So here are some alternatives. If the accusation is "You don't listen to me," you could say "Oh, I thought I was listening" because that's your truth. You thought you were listening. If the accusation is "You don't love me," you could say "I know in my heart that I love you" because that is your truth. Try to avoid any statement that involves telling the child what they think or know such as "You know I love you" because that can feel like an intrusive statement. Try to always speak from the first-person perspective. If the accusation is "You yell" and you don't believe that you do yell, then you would say "I didn't think I was yelling." If the accusation is that you don't cook food they like, do not remind them of how much they like your fish tacos or that they think you make the best lasagna around. You simply say "I thought that I was cooking food you liked."

If the accusation has anything to do with the other parent such as you're a bad husband or wife, it's your fault the marriage broke up, you're the one who's causing pain and suffering to the other parent, anything at all to do with the other parent, you should say something like "Well, I see that differently" "I have a different perspective on that," "I have a different understanding about that," or "I have a different memory of that," depending on the specifics.

Step five is a recap of the first three steps. You could say "Well, that didn't actually happen, but I understand that you think it's true and that you're very upset and angry about that. I want you to know I'm so grateful that you're sharing this with me because now I understand where you're coming from."

If the accusation is relevant for the future, not just the past, such as "You don't listen to me" and there could be multiple opportunities to listen going forward, you could end step five with an invitation such as "I invite you to tell me any time that you feel that I'm not listening, and I will stop what I'm doing and focus more on trying to understand what you're saying." If the accusation is that you yell, you could say "I invite you to tell me any time that you feel that my tone of voice is too loud or too intense, and I will speak more quietly." To be clear, you are not asking your child to provide you with examples of when this has happened in the past. For example, if the complaint is that you yell and you don't think that you do yell, don't ask your child to share with you three times when they think you yelled in the past. That will make the child feel that you are trying to trap them so that you can prove that they are wrong.

Reflections
- *Can you imagine feeling and expressing gratitude when your child complains to you?*
- *How comfortable are you noticing your child's emotional states?*
- *What do you need to do to be able to provide a one-sentence correction and refrain from drifting into a more in-depth explanation that provides your side of the story?*

USE THE MODIFIED FIVE STEPS FOR TRUE ACCUSATIONS

The next relevant scenario is when your child's accusation is at least partly true or mostly or even entirely true. If that's the case, you don't want to spend fifteen sentences going through the first three steps. That is just too long for the child to wait for you to acknowledge that you see the situation the same way they do.

In this case, what is recommended is a modified five steps where each of the first three steps is one or two sentences rather than five. So let's take as an example your child brings up a time when you slapped them when they were ten years old, and let's say that that actually happened. You definitely do not want to say to the child "Why can't you get over it already? I have already apologized. Why are you making such a big deal about it?"

This is where a modified five steps comes into use. Let's use as an example a fifteen-year-old child, Chris, who says "You slapped me when I was ten." You start with one sentence of gratitude to show your child that you are always grateful when they share their thoughts and feelings with you. It might sound like "Chris, thank you so much for telling me that you're thinking about that time when I slapped you when you were ten." Instead of five sentences of gratitude, you say just one sentence. Then you proceed to one sentence of compassion, noticing how the child is feeling in that very moment. You might say "I can see how upset it's making you feel thinking about that time." Then there is one sentence of expressed empathy, sounding something like "You know what? If I were a fifteen-year-old and I was remembering a time when my mom slapped me when I was ten, I might be pretty angry too." Remember to insert the actual emotion you have determined that your child is feeling. The emotion of anger is used here as just an example. In this way, steps one, two, and three—gratitude, compassion, and empathy—are rolled into one brief three-sentence opening.

Now step four would not involve a correction. Instead, it would be an acknowledgment that you have a shared understanding with the child that this in fact occurred. You might say "You know, I remember it the same way you do." It is essential when you acknowledge that you do not explain, justify, or minimize. Explaining would involve providing context about what was going on for you at the time. This might be something like "I had such a hard day at work and then I got stuck in traffic on the way home. If you knew how hard my day was, you would cut me some slack." Justification would involve contextual information about the behavior of the child you slapped to somehow make your slapping them more understandable, basically blaming the victim. An example might be "If you hadn't . . . I wouldn't have slapped you." And minimization is anything that tries to make the bad act not as bad such as "That was the only time" or "I didn't hit you that hard." The only exception to the no explaining, justifying, or minimizing is if your child asks you why you did what you did. Then you can respond with "Thank you so much for asking. I would be happy to tell you what was going on for me." But otherwise, you keep the focus on the child in the here and now.

Step five involves a sincere apology. You can simply say "I am so sorry that I did that." Again, do not offer any excuses or reasons because that detracts from the child's experience of the sincerity of the apology.

Step six involves your expressing a wish such as "If I could go back in time, I would do things differently"; "I wish that I had not done that"; or "If I could do things over again, I would always show you love and respect even when we are not seeing eye-to-eye." Sometimes children feel healed and comforted with the expression of a wish, even though it does not objectively change what has already happened.

Step seven involves your asking questions of your child, engaging in what we refer to as "compassionate curiosity." You are asking questions *because you care.* You could ask your child "What did that feel like for you at the time?" "What does it mean to you thinking back on that day now?" and "Is there anything else about that situation that you would like me to understand?" Remember that you are not asking questions to prove to the child that it wasn't really as bad as the child says such as "Well, did I leave any marks?" or "Can you think of any other time when that happened?" The questions aren't there to make the child see that they are wrong for being upset with you. The questions are there to show that you care because presumably you do care. Of course, if your child does share more thoughts and feelings, make sure to listen with your heart, avoid interrupting, and thank the child when they are done.

Many parents may balk at this idea of asking the child to share more of their thoughts and feelings about an incident that did not go well for the parent. You may also feel worried about probing the child's pain. You may be asking why you should invite your child to explore and expand on their complaints about you. You might be afraid that this will just make everything worse. You may be thinking that your child is mad enough as it is, so why should you "go there." The answer to these (understandable) questions is that there is a paradox here in that when you go *into* the pain, you can *heal* the pain. Perhaps you are familiar with an old-fashioned children's toy usually referred to as the finger trap. With this toy, you place a finger in either end of a tube and then try to get your fingers out of the tube. Intuitively, you pull your fingers *out*, but when you do that, the tube tightens and your fingers get stuck in the tube. But if you move your fingers toward the inside, then the tube relaxes and you can get your fingers out. This is an apt analogy in that if you try to pull away from the center of your child's pain, you get stuck, but if you can move toward it, things open up and relax and there is a path forward.

Reflections

- *How can you avoid going into a shame spiral when your child brings up a legitimate complaint against you?*

- *How can you avoid feeling frustrated if your child brings up the same complaint you thought you had already apologized for?*

- *What do you need to do to be able to listen to your child's thoughts and feelings without sharing your side of the story?*

There are four final points relevant to the five steps and the modified five steps. The first is that you might realize after the fact that you missed an opportunity to use the five steps. Please do not be too hard on yourself. None of this is obvious or intuitive. Fortunately, you can always go back to a topic and ask for a do-over. You can say to your child "Hey, remember last night/last week/ten minutes ago when you shared that you were upset about [insert the child's complaint] and I responded by getting defensive. That is not how I want to respond. What I really want to say is ..." and then launch into the five steps or modified five steps depending on the accusation at hand. There is no rule that says that if you missed an opportunity you have to just live with that.

Second, if your child comments or complains that you sound different or like you got coached, please do not get defensive about that. There is nothing to be ashamed about. We recommend that you own it as a point of pride. "Yes! I probably do sound different. That's because I am learning all sorts of new ways to talk to you kids because nothing is more important to me than getting our relationship back on track. I am always going to keep growing and learning as a parent. Hopefully, you will see the benefits of that effort!" You do not have to feel that you got caught red-handed doing something bad, wrong, or shameful.

Third, if you are worried that you will forget the five steps, you can write them down on a piece of paper and refer to the paper when you are speaking with your child. You can say "I made some notes about how I wanted to handle it the next time you raised an issue with me." There is nothing to be ashamed of. You have nothing to hide. You can tape them onto the fridge or keep them on your phone as a friendly reminder.

And finally, if you use these steps many times, they may get repetitive and start to sound like you are on autopilot, which is not the message you want to convey. At that point, you can say "You know the drill. First, I am going to thank you for sharing and letting me know what is on your mind." And you can actually do step one and express your gratitude. And then you can say "And now I am going to really pay attention to how it feels for you . . ." and so forth. You can do the steps but also acknowledge that your child probably recognizes that you have a method to responding to their complaints.

AVOID FALSE ALLEGATIONS OF CHILD ABUSE OR NEGLECT

Of course, you do not have control over what the other parent or someone else does and says about you. At the same time, there are things you should know to do or not do that will make it much harder for someone to make a false allegation of child maltreatment against you. There are four major types of child maltreatment, each of which will be briefly described along with examples of behaviors to make sure that you do or do not do to reduce the likelihood that a false allegation will be made against you.

What many people do not know is that in general, the child protection system is authorized to remove a child from your home. What that means is if there is an allegation made against you and it is screened in as being worthy of being investigated, the child protection worker can remove a child from your home while there's an investigation going on. Once the investigation is over, generally, the child protection system submits a letter saying that the result is unfounded—meaning there is no finding of abuse or neglect—and then they withdraw their attention from your family. It is not automatic that your parenting time would be resumed. Often, what happens is the parent who was investigated has to ask the other parent to resume parenting time and if that parent refuses to do so, then you would have to file a motion with the court to ask the court to intervene and make that other parent resume your parenting time. That often results in the other parent filing a response motion claiming that the child does not want to go back. At that point, the court is obligated to consider what is in the child's best interest. And if the other parent can make a legitimate claim that it's better for the child to not be returned to you and not have your parenting time resumed, then that is what will happen. So even though your child was removed for, in essence, no reason, you still may not have your parenting time resumed. In an ideal situation, if there is a false allegation made against you, it would be so clear that it's unfounded from the start so that it would either be screened out or the initial investigation would result in a closing of the case before your child is removed from your care. Thus, the more you know about the different types of maltreatment and all the behaviors to avoid, the better off you will be. It is also important to be aware of the fact that each state has a different definition of the different types of maltreatment. What is presented below represents general definitions, but it is always best to consult your own state's laws to ensure that you have the most relevant definitions and standards for your situation. The Child Welfare Information Gateway (https://www.childwelfare.gov/topics/can/defining/) is an excellent source for this information.

Physical Abuse
Physical abuse is generally defined as nonaccidental injury or harm to the child that was inflicted by the parent. Examples of physical abuse include hitting, punching, or grabbing a child

harshly in a way that causes an injury; or pulling a child's hair or twisting their arm. The truth is, however, that if your child were injured or claimed to be injured by you even if it were an accident, it could still result in a physical abuse claim against you. For example, if your child refuses to turn off their cell phone when you ask and you respond by grabbing the phone out of their hand and the child falls and bumps their head, that could result in a physical abuse claim against you even though it was clearly an accident. If you roughly pick up a child who is behaving badly and put them firmly on their bed for a time-out and the child claimed or experienced that as your throwing them on the bed, you could get a physical abuse claim against you. Here, the point is that the distinction between accidental and nonaccidental injury is not always clear.

The best way to avoid a physical abuse claim against you, therefore, is to never touch your child in anger. For example, if your child is sitting on the couch and you ask them many times to clear the table and they do not do so, do not go over to that child and take their hands and pull them up from a sitting position on the couch to direct them over to the kitchen to clear the table. You could be accused of yanking your child, perhaps even dislocating their shoulder or causing semipermanent damage to their arms. Sometimes when we're angry, we cannot tell how hard we are touching someone. To avoid accidentally engaging in physical abuse and being accused of engaging in physical abuse, the safest thing to do is simply not to touch your child in anger. Obviously, this includes spanking. As noted elsewhere in this book, it is better to tell the child that you're upset with them and say that you will deal with it later rather than respond in the heat of the moment and make a terrible mistake. If a child protection worker did come to investigate a claim of physical abuse, it would be best if you could honestly say to them "I never touch my child in anger." That would be better than having to explain a convoluted story about how you were just grabbing the phone out of your child's hand and they fell down and hit their head. Even if that does eventually result in your being cleared from an abuse charge, you have revealed that you are not an effective parent, and you could get mandated to take parenting classes. Even that can cause a stain on your record in the eyes of the court and can certainly reinforce to the child that there is something problematic about you as a parent. For suggestions on nonphysical discipline strategies, please see Chapter 4.

Reflections

- *Have you relied on physical punishment in the past, and are you ready to find new discipline strategies?*
- *Do you feel that you already have the self-control to avoid situations that could cause harm to your child, and if not, what do you need to be there?*

Sexual Abuse

Sexual abuse is defined as sexual interaction imposed on a person and includes both contact (i.e., touching, fondling, and penetration) and noncontact (i.e., exposing oneself or having the other person expose themselves). As with other forms of child maltreatment, there are many parental behaviors that could be misconstrued to be sexually abusive. Here are some things to keep in mind to reduce the likelihood that a false sexual abuse allegation could be made against you.

First, reduce nudity between you and your child. Do not take showers or baths together. Once the child is over a certain age, they can be taught to wash themselves in the bath so that there would be no need for you to touch their private parts. The basic rule is not to touch them where the bathing suit goes (top and bottom, front and back). Again, once your child is old enough, they can wipe themselves after going to the bathroom, and you should not need to be touching them there. Avoid nudity on your part. Close your bedroom door when you are changing.

Don't walk from the bathroom to the bedroom with just a towel wrapped around you because the towel could fall down and you could be accused of exposing yourself to your child.

Second, don't introduce sexual content into the relationship. Don't comment on your child's sexual development in a salacious manner, and don't have any pornography around (printed material or on your phone). If you rub your child's back at night, make sure to stay on the back and not go anywhere near the waistband of their pajamas. If you lie down with the child at night, it is best if you are not under the covers. If you have a sexual partner, make sure that your children don't see that person naked or hear or see the two of you having sex.

Third, avoid high-risk situations. Specifically, if your partner is a male, make sure not to leave them alone with your children, especially young girls. A nonbiological male molesting a young girl represents the archetypal sexual abuse scenario, and many people would assume that that person is guilty. With sexual abuse, it is very hard to prove that it happened, and it is also very hard to disprove that it happened. Thus, once an allegation has been made, it is hard to get the stain, or the appearance of guilt, off of you. It is far better to not do anything that could in any way be misconstrued as sexual. Once your child reaches prepuberty, it is wise to get an approved book on adolescence and puberty so that you can talk to your child about healthy sexual development in a way that is 100 percent aboveboard and beyond reproach.

Reflections

- *Do the recommendations here feel consistent with your parenting strategies already, and if not, what can you do to get there?*

- *Are there other ways that you can protect yourself from a false allegation of sexual abuse?*

Physical Neglect

The narrow definition of physical neglect is a failure to provide food, clothing, and shelter for your child. However, there are many parenting behaviors that fall under a subcategory of physical neglect referred to as inadequate guardianship. This generally refers to harm that comes to your child because you failed to protect them. You can think about these parenting behaviors as things that happen inside the home, outside the home, and in the car. With respect to things that happen inside the home, what you need to keep in mind is that if your child gets hurt because you failed to provide a safe home environment, then you are guilty of neglect, specifically inadequate guardianship. If you have a bottle of whiskey on top of your refrigerator and your child drags a chair over to the refrigerator, climbs up, gets the whiskey, drinks it, and gets alcohol poisoning, you could be guilty of inadequate guardianship because your child got sick based on your failure to remove the whiskey from the environment. If you wake up on Sunday morning and your child is making eggs at the stove and gets burned, you are guilty of neglect because your child got hurt because you failed to provide adequate supervision for them. To avoid an allegation of inadequate guardianship, you should start by walking through your home—every single room—and "neglect proof" it. People baby proof their home, but they fail to consider the things they need to do to protect their child from harm as their children grow. Walk through each room of your home, and check whether you have carbon monoxide and smoke detectors in each room, a fire extinguisher in the kitchen, and a fire safety plan. Determine whether there is alcohol or prescription medication in easy reach that would be dangerous for your child to access. Ask yourself whether you need to teach your children how to use the stove when you're not around, which knives are safe for them to use, and how to use the microwave. Walk through your entire home and make sure that it is safe for your children. Another aspect of home safety has to do with how old children need to be to be left home alone. Make sure that you know what the law is so that you don't inadvertently break it by leaving a child who is too young home alone. In that situation, your child might not need to get hurt for you to be guilty of inadequate guardianship. All that would need to happen is your child revealing to somebody that they were left home alone and you could get in trouble. But even if your child is old enough to meet the legal requirements of staying home alone, you might decide that your child is not safe to be home alone. Some children are more mischievous, curious, adventurous, thrill seeking, and rule breaking. You know your child. If you believe that your child is likely to come into harm's way because you left them home alone, then don't do it even if they're old enough by law.

Inadequate guardianship outside the home primarily refers to whether your children are wearing helmets and the proper padding for when they are skateboarding, rollerblading, or riding their bicycle. With respect to the car, make sure that your car seats are up to legal safety standards; don't let your children sit up front until they're old enough or weigh enough, depending on the state law; don't let them share seat belts in the back; and don't drink and drive, text and drive, or speed. You cannot afford to cut any safety corners.

Reflections

- *How does it feel to think that you need to be so careful with every aspect of your home life and parenting?*

- *In what ways does being this vigilant to protect your children from harm feel helpful to you, and in what ways does it feel unhelpful?*

Psychological Maltreatment

Psychological maltreatment is the formal term for what is generally referred to as emotional abuse or neglect (Hart et al., 2017). There are six main types of psychological maltreatment: spurning (i.e., rejecting, degrading, or humiliating); terrorizing (i.e., frightening the child or threatening to abandon or harm the child or the child's loved ones); isolating (i.e., preventing the child from having freedom of movement or ability to socialize); exploiting/corrupting (i.e., allowing, modeling, or encouraging the child to engage in behaviors that warp their development); denying emotional responsiveness (i.e., failing to provide love, affection, warmth, and attention); and failing to provide medical, mental health, or educational services to the child. Although there are many types and subtypes of psychological maltreatment, for the purposes of this book, only a few will be highlighted. More detailed and comprehensive information is provided on the Psychological Maltreatment Alliance website (www.psychologicalmaltreatment.org).

For our purposes, make sure that you do not behave in an unkind or rejecting manner. That means do not speak sarcastically to your child, do not have cruel and mocking nicknames for them, and do not embarrass them in front of their peers or on social media. Avoid frightening or terrorizing your child by threatening to harm them or someone or something that they love. Avoid modeling or encouraging antisocial behavior, such as smoking, vaping, drinking, having pornography, truancy, and bullying, and don't rely on your children for emotional support. Avoid saying things such as you cannot live without them, you are so lonely without them, you are the only one who understands them, or other self-serving and manipulative statements. Also avoid involving them in any disputes that you might be having with their other parent or other people who are important to them.

Reflections
- *Do you feel that you have clarity about this form of child maltreatment, or do you want to learn more about it?*
- *Does it feel comfortable for you to commit to avoiding behaviors that could be construed as psychological maltreatment?*

SOME LIKELY TROUBLE SPOTS

There are certain issues that are likely to be problematic for you and your child because they are common trouble spots in many parent–child relationships and they can easily be exploited in situations with hurt, angry, rejecting, distant children. The first is chores, the second is cell phones, and the third is cleaning their room.

With respect to chores, we concur with the general belief that it is good for children to participate in the upkeep of the household and to learn basic skills (e.g., washing dishes, setting the table, and making a bed). Our concern is that if your child is already hurt, angry, rejecting, and distant, it is possible that arguments over chores will become flashpoints for increased conflict and negativity in the relationship. Things to keep in mind are inviting your child's cooperation rather than assigning chores, being proactive by teaching your child the skills to do the chore, engaging in family meeting discussions to develop a shared agreement about chores, and mutual problem solving when something isn't going right. More information about these positive parenting strategies can be found in Chapter 4.

Arguments over cell phones are rampant in families with hurt, angry, rejecting, distant children, especially if the child's feelings are being engendered by the other parent in a conflicted separation/divorce situation. To avoid escalation of conflict, never grab the phone out of the child's hand, and try as much as possible to develop agreed-upon rules for phone usage in the home. Family meeting and mutual problem solving are going to be useful here as well. Ideally, discussions about phone rules and phone safety can occur prior to the child having a phone.

Likewise, there is likely to be disagreement around a child not cleaning their room. This typically emerges as a problem when the child becomes a teenager. Try to think in advance about what the most important aspects of the situation are for you, such as no eating in the room to prevent bugs from coming into the house. You and your child can discuss everything else (i.e., what a clean room is, how often should it be cleaned, and who does the cleaning). There is really no absolute right or wrong (other than cleanliness issues), and you want to avoid moralistically condemning your child's preference for having clothes strewn around the room. Try to remember that this is most likely a phase that they will outgrow.

At the end of the day, it is always a priority for you to avoid engaging in behaviors that unnecessarily exacerbate your child feeling hurt, angry, rejecting, and distant from you. You always want your child to feel that you are on their team, rooting for them, wanting for them what they want for themselves. You want to make sure that you don't take the bait and act as if something is more important than your love for them.

Reflections

- *What parenting issues are likely to be conflicted for you and your child? What can you do now to prepare yourself to handle these issues in a loving manner?*

- *Can you remember what it felt like as a child to feel that your parent was being too hard on you? What did you wish your parent had done or said to assure you that they were on your side?*

CHAPTER THREE

Foster Four Values

THE NEXT STRATEGY INVOLVES INSTILLING AND FOSTERING FOUR specific values in your child. These four values are particularly relevant for protecting your child from becoming further hurt, angry, rejecting, and distant: forgiveness, compassion, integrity, and critical thinking. In addition to the suggestions presented below, you may want to consider giving your child a copy of *Getting Through My Parents' Divorce* (Baker & Andre, 2015) because there is a chapter in the workbook focused on core values and what they mean to children. The workbook is designed especially for middle school children who are caught in a loyalty conflict, so it may or may not be appropriate for your situation. Other hurt, angry, rejecting, distant children (i.e., those not caught in a loyalty conflict) might benefit from some of the activities, and you may want to simply direct your child to specific pages in the book. Obviously, careful thought needs to be given to how to offer the workbook to your child because you don't want to appear to be implying or assuming that the other parent is responsible for the conflict in your relationship with your child. You may even want to copy just a few pages out of the workbook and give them to your child to focus them on the specific issue of clarifying their values.

Forgiveness

The first relevant value is forgiveness. Forgiveness is particularly relevant for conflicted family situations because all parents are imperfect. All parents hurt, frustrate, and disappoint their children. And if your child comes to believe that you have engaged in a behavior that is *unforgivable*, then your child is well on the road to cutting you off or at least maintaining their hurt, angry, rejecting, and distant stance. The goal is not for you to be perfect; although that would be great, it's not possible. The goal is for you to be the best possible parent you can be and then to have your child accept you with your imperfections and be able to forgive you when you do something that hurts, frustrates, or disappoints them. If your child believes that you have engaged in a behavior that is unforgivable, then your child will be much more likely to cut you off. Thankfully, there are ways to foster the value of forgiveness in your child.

The first is if your child naturally exhibits forgiveness toward somebody else, then you want to highlight it by using the word *forgiveness* and commending, praising, and appreciating your child for demonstrating forgiveness. For example, if you have two children and one was annoyed, hurt, angry, or frustrated with their sibling and then forgives that sibling and does something nice for that child who earlier had been so annoying, then you can say to your child, "Wow, your sister was really bugging you earlier, but it looks like you've forgiven her and now decided to share your cupcake with her. I wonder how that feels for you. I know that I'm impressed and proud of you." So instead of just saying to your child "That's nice that you are sharing your cupcake" or "Good girl for sharing your cupcake," you are being very specific about the value that your child is exhibiting and praising and recognizing your child when they demonstrate that value spontaneously. Certainly, if your child forgives *you* for something you have done, you can thank your child. Imagine that you promised to get Chinese food on the way home from work but you forgot, were too busy, or ran late and you show up without the Chinese food that your child had been looking forward to enjoying. If your child responds by saying something like "That's okay, Mom/Dad. I know you will get it next time," then you can say in response "Wow, thank you for forgiving me. I really appreciate it. I'm noticing how flexible and thoughtful you are being. I am so proud of you." Again, you're using the word *forgiveness* and thereby helping your child develop an identity as somebody who has forgiveness in their repertoire.

You can also talk out loud as you demonstrate forgiveness throughout the day. An example might be if you are driving in the car with your child and somebody cuts you off. Instead of venting your anger, you can speak out loud and say "Boy, that driver really irked me, but I'm going to forgive him. I'm not going to carry that around because that just makes me feel bad." Additionally, if you're watching a movie or reading a book together with your child and a character is struggling with the decision about whether to forgive somebody, you can ask your child what they think that character should do or what they would do if they were in that situation. You can also demonstrate forgiveness toward your child by saying "You know, I'm really upset that you did [whatever the child did] earlier, but I forgive you. I'm going to let that go because that will feel better for both of us." And then you can ask your child how that feels to be forgiven and to acknowledge that the world is a better place when people forgive each other.

Reflections

- *How does it feel to forgive someone who has hurt you?*
- *Do you worry that your child will not forgive you for something real or imagined that you did?*
- *What do you feel are the essential elements of forgiveness?*

COMPASSION

The second relevant value is compassion. This is relevant specifically for parenting a child who is hurt, angry, rejecting, and distant because these children can come to believe that your feelings do not matter and/or that they are entitled to treat you poorly because you deserve it. If your child has come to believe that your feelings don't matter, then they are much more likely to behave in a harsh and unkind way toward you, to be demeaning or contemptuous of you, or to not factor in your feelings and basic humanity when interacting with you or making decisions. Likewise, you don't want your child to break your heart or treat you as if your feelings don't matter, so you want to foster in your child a belief that compassion is an important value. Ideally, your child will manifest an identity as somebody who values and has compassion.

The ways that you can foster compassion in your child are to recognize when your child spontaneously exhibits compassion and praise and appreciate your child for doing so. You can discuss your own feelings of compassion for your child. If your child looks sad, for example, you can say "I feel compassion for you right now. I am noticing what you're feeling." If your child has an ethical dilemma about how to respond to a situation, you can ask your child to consider how to resolve this in a way that is compassionate toward the other person. You can ask your child for compassion such as by saying "I'm stressed right now. I need some compassion from you." And if you see characters in books and movies engaging in compassionate behaviors or having dilemmas where they don't know whether they want to or will be able to be compassionate, you can discuss it with your child.

Reflections

- *When is it hard to feel compassion for your child or for yourself?*

- *How can you manage your hurt when your child disregards your feelings?*

- *Can you try to hold onto the idea that becoming compassionate is a process and many children have lapses just because they are young and not fully developed?*

INTEGRITY

The third value that's relevant for hurt, angry, rejecting, distant children is integrity, defined loosely as acting in a manner that is consistent with one's values and truth. The opposite would involve being unduly influenced by somebody else to behave in a way that goes against your values. If your child has integrity, it will be harder for them to become convinced that they don't love you, you don't love them, or you are dangerous or unavailable when that is not the case. You want your child to know who you are based on how you relate to them, not based on what somebody else is communicating to your child about who you are. And you want your child to relate to you in a way that's based on the values of forgiveness and compassion, so integrity is a vital value for your child to possess.

The way that you foster integrity is to acknowledge and recognize when your child exhibits integrity by being true to themselves and others. For example, if your child values learning and honesty and chooses to study hard when cheating would be possible or chooses being kind when doing so has no obvious reward to the child but simply because that's what the child values, then notice and comment on that. Any time you see your child demonstrating what you would consider to be integrity, you can acknowledge that in the child. You can say "You have exhibited integrity right there. You could have gone a different way. You made the tough choice, but I think that you made the right choice for you. How do you feel about your choice?"

Reflections
- *What are some of your child's core values, and how can you continue to reinforce them?*
- *How can you be a role model of integrity for your child?*

CRITICAL THINKING

The fourth value is critical thinking, defined as the objective analysis and evaluation of an issue or idea to form a rational judgment. It is an active and deliberate process that involves considering the evidence rather than making an emotional decision or judgment based on feelings, biases, and assumptions. This is highly relevant for hurt, angry, rejecting, distant children because often they are acting on an emotional and unexamined set of ideas and feelings about who you are and what you mean to them. To the extent that these unexamined thoughts and feelings are implanted by someone else and are distortions, then the child will be reacting to you based on false ideas rather than on reality. Further, if the assumptions and beliefs remain unexamined, the child may not even be aware of them. A complicating factor is that most people do not like to be told that they are being manipulated or acting on distorted ideas. It is generally insulting to tell someone that they are being irrational. So offhanded or not well-thought-out attempts to undo false ideas can backfire and actually reinforce what started out as a lie or a distortion (see Chapter 2, "Don't Take the Bait").

That doesn't mean that there is nothing to be done. The goal is to nurture critical thinking skills about topics unrelated to your child's thoughts and feelings about you. This can then transfer over to other settings and situations. In addition to the suggestions presented below, you may want to consider giving your child a copy of *Getting Through My Parents' Divorce* (Baker & Andre, 2015) because there is a chapter in the workbook on developing critical thinking skills in children. As noted earlier, the workbook is designed especially for middle school children who are caught in a loyalty conflict, so it may or may not be appropriate for your situation. Other hurt, angry, rejecting, distant children (i.e., those not caught in a loyalty conflict) might benefit from some of the activities, and you may want to simply direct your child to specific pages in the book. Obviously, careful thought needs to be given to how to offer the workbook to your child because you don't want to appear to be thinking or assuming that the other parent is responsible for the conflict in your relationship with your child. You may even want to copy just a few pages out of the handbook and give them to your child to focus them on the specific issue of developing critical thinking skills.

Some other ways to encourage critical thinking skills include asking your child when they make a declarative statement such as product A is better than product B, it is a good idea to cram for a test, or it doesn't matter about being nice to people because it's a dog-eat-dog world or any sort of declarative statement. Rather than responding with "Oh, that's a great idea" or "Oh, that's not true" and inserting your opinion on these topics, it is recommend that you respond by saying "That's an interesting idea; how did you come to that?" You can then follow up by asking questions in a friendly and openhearted way. It's not about attacking or challenging your child or making them feel that they have a ridiculous, stupid, or wrong idea. The focus should not be on what *you* think of the child's idea at all. It's about acknowledging that your child has an idea and being interested in how they came to that idea. You are asking your child to share, not defend.

Another way to instill critical thinking skills in your child is to engage in mutual problem solving. If you and your child do not see eye-to-eye on something, whether it be allowance or bedtime, rather than taking a "it's my way or the highway" approach or "well, it's your life; do whatever you want" approach, you could say to the child "Gee, we don't seem to agree about this. You think X is a good idea and I think Y is the way to go. How do you think we can find a solution that we both feel good about?" By responding this way, you are showing your child that there are at least two perspectives on a particular problem or situation and that that is okay. You don't always have to agree, because you are two separate people. You can then invite your child to brainstorm solutions. This is not the same as compromising, which often results in just splitting the difference. Brainstorming involves creative problem solving to come up with a solution that you both like. That process involves critical and creative thinking skills to avoid getting locked into the obvious solutions. The goal is to find something that truly feels good for both of you.

Yet another way to endorse critical thinking skills is to ask your child to consider various options when she shares a problem with you. For example, your child might say "I'm going to fail my math test tomorrow." Instead of just saying "Oh, that's not true," "Well, you should have studied more," or "That's the worst thing ever! That's a catastrophe. We can't have that," you could start by saying to your child "What do you think about that?" and asking "Do you have an idea of what you want to do about that?" That way you are inviting your child to think about choices and options. "What are things you could do since it's six o'clock now and your test is tomorrow morning?" Rather than telling them what to do, you are encouraging your child to think of choices for themselves and consider those choices. You want to avoid the idea that there is only one solution to a problem.

This is a very important element of dealing with hurt, angry, rejecting, distant children because your child could feel pressure from the other parent to act a certain way toward you and you want your child to be able to consider options rather than just caving in to that pressure, for example, if the other parent says to your child "Just call your [other parent] and tell them that you're not coming tomorrow" or "Call your [other parent] and tell them not to show up at your soccer game." Much of the time children feel like they must do what their parent tells them to do, especially in the heat of the moment. And of course, your child could be getting pressure from some source other than the other parent such as an older sibling or peers, even sometimes a person in authority such as a coach who has the intention to disrupt your relationship with your child. Regardless of where the pressure may be coming from, your goal is to help your child understand that in most situations, there are choices to consider; then you can help the child figure out how to not always give in to the pressure to cut off or demean you. You want to take advantage of natural opportunities to encourage your child to consider options. Rather than your telling the child what to do, ask your child "What are you thinking about doing? What are some approaches you're considering?" or "What are your plans?" If you take this approach, be sure to ask these types of questions in a loving and connected way. You don't want to imply that the child has to figure it all out on their own. You are asking questions in a loving and connected manner to hear what they are thinking. Your tone of voice and facial expression should be conveying loving interest and availability.

A modern-day manifestation of the need for critical thinking is the easy access everyone has to information online that may seem to be accurate or coming from an authoritative source but can really be propaganda, lies, and misinformation. Any time your child declares that they learned something online, you can ask your child what the source was for that information, and then you can show them how to discern the credibility of sources. Just because something looks and sounds definitive and official does not actually mean that it is accurate.

A final example of how to instill critical thinking skills in your child is to help them make a pros and cons list. If your child has a difficult decision or choice to make (e.g., whether to drop an instrument or sport in high school, whether to spend their birthday gift money or save it, or whether to forgive a friend for a hurtful transgression), you can teach your child how to consider all the potential reasons to make one choice and all of the potential reasons to not make that choice. You can teach your child that sometimes people make rash or impulsive decisions without considering all the angles. You can model doing this for your child and explain that at first it seemed like you were leaning in one direction but when you made your pros and cons list, it helped you realize that in fact the other way to go made more sense.

The bottom line is that you want to try to imbue in your child an ability to think about thinking, which can help protect the child against behaving in a hurt, angry, rejecting, and distant manner toward you. Remember that as tempting as it can be, you don't want your child adopting somebody else's view, even if it's a view in which you happen to agree. For example, if your child says to you that "Cheating is wrong, so I'm not going to cheat," you might be relieved. But you don't want to miss the opportunity to say "That's a fascinating idea, and I would love to hear more about that. Walk me through how you came to that." In doing so, you can teach your child that conclusions don't just pop up out of nowhere. They're based on values, beliefs, knowledge, reasoning, and facts. You want to help your child make that connection so that they do not just one day say that you're somehow unsavory or bad but not be able to explain the source of that thought.

Reflections

- *What are some opportunities to teach your child critical thinking skills?*
- *Are there times in which you could benefit from being more critical in your own decision making?*

Chapter Four

Be a Positive Parent

Positive parenting is a catch-all phrase for a philosophy of parenting that draws upon the principles of human relationships, written about by Alfred Adler (1927), Dreikurs (1991), and Nelson (2006), and styles of parenting, as identified by psychologist Diana Baumrind (1966). Although there is no one perfect consensus definition, the core concepts of positive parenting are exemplified in the following eight principles: (1) promote a secure attachment, (2) teach respect by being respectful, (3) be proactive, (4) engage in reflective parenting, (5) use emotion coaching to teach self-regulation, (6) be encouraging, (7) invite cooperation, and (8) use positive discipline strategies. Each of these core concepts involves several specific strategies.

Promote a Secure Attachment

The quality of the attachment relationship between parent and child is the foundational experience for children and sets the stage for their personality and behavior as they develop. Promoting a secure attachment begins in infancy with parents providing loving touch, predictably meeting basic needs, and conveying warmth and affection. Children whose parents promote a secure attachment in infancy grow up to be happier, more cooperative, and more receptive to parental guidance. Even as children mature past infancy and the early attachment relationship has been formed, there are many ways parents can continue to promote a secure attachment bond with their children. And these aspects of parenting are essential for children who—for whatever reason—become hurt, angry, rejecting, and distant.

There are five specific strategies for promoting a secure attachment with a hurt, angry, rejecting, distant child: (1) Always be safe, loving, and available; (2) stay connected and available even when the child is upset; (3) stay near an upset child; (4) spend undirected quality time every day; and (5) don't shame the child for having normal needs and emotions.

Be Safe, Loving, and Available

As noted earlier in this part of the book, being safe, loving, and available is the cornerstone of a healthy and happy parent–child relationship. When children feel that their parent is safe, loving, and available, they are more likely to be cooperative, listen to parental guidance, and be pleasant to be with. That loving bond provides the basis for all other interactions and sets the stage for a well-behaved and competent child. Practically speaking, this means touching and talking to your child in a soothing and predictable manner, responding to their cues (cries, requests for help, signals that they are uncomfortable or hungry or frightened) in a timely and predictable manner, and playing with and spending time with your child in a way that includes shared positive moments together. Avoid being frightening, unpredictable, and harsh because these behaviors disrupt the attachment and reduce the likelihood that your child will feel good about themselves or you. If your child does not trust that you are going to be kind and available, then your child will be less likely to be cooperative and to adhere to your guidance.

Relationship expert Gottman coined the phrase the "magic ratio" to remind people to express five affirmative statements for every one criticism for a person to feel satisfied in a relationship.

While this ratio was first identified in adult romantic relationships, it is recommended here that a similar ratio be applied to parental communications to children. Your child—especially one who is hurt, angry, rejecting, and distant—needs to feel affirmed and loved by you, their parent. Try to remember that every day your child needs to hear compliments, praise, and appreciation. One trap that parents in your situation can fall into is having most parent–child interactions be negative, with you reprimanding and scolding your child. This barrage of negativity reinforces the child's perception that you are not loving, and it can induce in you a feeling of hopelessness and despair about the relationship.

Try to remember when making compliments that you vary them, sometimes focusing on external attributes ("your hair style really looks nice today" or "what a colorful outfit; you look like a summer garden") and internal attributes ("thank you for [insert task]; that was so helpful" or "I see how hard you are working to finish that project").

Reflections

- *When is it hard for you to be safe, loving, and available to your child?*

- *What work can you do on yourself to enhance your capacity to be safe, loving, and available?*

- *What are positive aspects of your child's personality and character that you can appreciate?*

Stay Connected and Available Even When the Child Is Upset

Part of promoting a secure attachment is remaining connected to the child even when the child is misbehaving or being unpleasant (having a temper tantrum, being disrespectful, not cooperating). Children need to know that their parent is emotionally available even when their behavior is less than ideal. What this means in practical terms is that you show empathy for your child when they are having a hard time and you convey that you are there for them. This involves noticing that the child is upset and being emotionally available and not rejecting the child for their negative emotions. For example, you might say, "I see you are upset. Let's talk about what's going on," rather than saying, "Be pleasant," "Stop frowning," or "Don't be such a sour puss." Let the child know that you see that they are upset and you care about what is going on. Sometimes there are certain things that upset a child that can be particularly annoying to the parent such as a seemingly unreasonable attachment to an object, an embarrassing difficulty sharing with other children, or behavior that belies a sense of entitlement and lack of empathy for others. Perhaps it is misbehavior in front of other people whom the parent feels are judging them. Sometimes the child's behavior triggers a memory or feeling in the parent of their own frustrations and disappointment carried over from their own childhood. In these instances, it is necessary for you, the parent, to work past your own frustration, annoyance, or embarrassment about your child's behavior to stay connected.

Reflections
- *What are some things that are upsetting for your child?*
- *How do you generally feel when your child is upset?*
- *What can you do or say to yourself to help you stay connected even when your child is upset?*

Stay Near an Upset Child
Many parents are moving away from the use of time-out as a discipline strategy because it involves the withdrawal of parental support and nurturance at a time when the child is most in need of loving reassurance. Instead, many positive parenting proponents are suggesting a "time-in" during which the parent provides loving guidance and support for the child during a difficult time. The parent is providing an external structure (by holding the child—if the child wants to be held—and comforting the child with loving

compassion) when the child is not able to provide that structure and control for themselves. You may adopt the concept of DEAR Time (drop everything and replenish) as discussed in Chapter 1.

Reflections

- *How would it feel to hug and nurture your child instead of sending them to a time-out or punishing them?*

- *What are some things you could say to your child when they are upset to show that you care about them?*

Spend Undirected Quality Time Every Day

Children need at least twenty minutes of their parent's absolute undivided attention every day engaging in what is referred to as "undirected play." That term refers to any activity the child chooses in which the child takes the lead, without the parent providing direction, structure, teaching, or feedback. For example, if you and your child are drawing together, you would not make suggestions or corrections ("Let's color the cow brown" or "You know grass is not purple"). You are there to be an observer and partner rather than teacher or guide. You follow the child's lead. Often this can be boring for the parent who may have chores or work to get done, or even entertainment/relaxation that seems more compelling, but it is vital for children's feeling of closeness and connection to you that you engage in this kind of activity every day. During these moments, you should stay away from all distractions such as cell phones and devote your full attention to your child.

Reflections

- *How would it feel to set aside all distractions and focus all your undivided attention on your child?*

- *How would it feel to refrain from making suggestions about the "right" way to do something?*

- *Can you commit to spending twenty minutes a day with your child in this way?*

Don't Shame the Child for Having Normal Needs and Emotions
Children have many needs, whether they are an infant's need to
be cleaned and fed, a toddler's need to make choices, a tween's
need for socialization, or a teen's need for privacy. Children are
also hardwired to have certain automatic responses such as crying when they fall or are frightened or laughing when they are
amused or tickled. A secure attachment is promoted when parents
acknowledge and address their children's needs and emotions
without shaming or blaming the child. It can disrupt the security
of the attachment if the parent conveys to the child that their
normal expressions of needs and feelings are disgusting, inappro-
priate, greedy, or harmful. For example, if your child makes a mess
by smearing chocolate on their face and seems to be enjoying the
tactile sensation, don't frown or scold the child or tell them that
they are bad for making a mess. You can smile and comment that
it seems like they are really enjoying the feeling of chocolate on
their hands and face. You can delight in their delight. Then you
can calmly wash the child or provide them with a washcloth to
wipe their face when they are ready.

Likewise, if your child cries because something is frightening
them, please do not laugh at their reaction; it is not something
that is in their control, and it is not something that a child should
feel ashamed about. And certainly do not do something intentionally to frighten your child and then take pleasure in their
reaction. For example, you might hold a smartphone up for your
child and then activate a filter that creates the impression that a
spider is crawling across their face. You may know that it is not
real, but a young child does not have the life experience to discern
the difference between reality and a phone filter. We strongly recommend that you do not show your children frightening filters or
do anything else to intentionally frighten your child and—if they
do become frightened by something—do not respond as if their
fear is amusing to you. Your child should not feel that their pain
and suffering are entertaining to you because that creates a breach
in the attachment bond.

Reflections
- *What are some feelings or needs your child has that you may find embarrassing or uncomfortable?*
- *What can you do or say to yourself to help you stay connected even when your child is expressing these needs or feelings?*

Teach Respect by Being Respectful

Children who are hurt, angry, rejecting, and distant often behave in a way that is described by the parent as "disrespectful." Although labels are best avoided when it comes to describing the behavior of children, what these parents generally mean when they say their child is disrespectful is that the child is behaving in a way that conveys contempt for the parent. They can convey contempt through their facial expressions (e.g., eye rolling); verbalizations (name-calling, sarcasm, and hostile verbal rejection); and body posture (turning away while the parent is speaking). Needless to say, this feels bad for the parent who misses their once loving, affectionate, cooperative child. Parents also worry that if their child behaves that way toward them, that they will behave this way toward other people and thereby have a hard time getting along with peers, colleagues, and eventually romantic partners.

One way to prevent this kind of behavior from developing in your child is to make sure that you as the parent consistently refrain from engaging in any of these behaviors yourself. Children have a right to be treated with respect and dignity even if you are displeased with their behavior. When your child feels respected, they are motivated to do better. It is essential to remember that there is always a polite, calm, friendly way to speak with your child and that doing so—especially when frustrated, hurt, angry, or upset yourself—allows you to be a role model for your child of what respectful communication is all about. Bearing this in mind will lead you to avoid speaking with sarcasm, using cruel or embarrassing nicknames, or being harsh and demeaning toward your child. It may help you to practice being calm and loving toward your child and speaking with calmness and respect even while your child is pushing your buttons. It may help to practice the techniques for managing your emotional arousal (see Chapter 2 about learning how to regulate your emotions).

Examples of respectful communication for when a child wants something that the parent does not necessarily agree with include "I understand you would like to stay up late tonight. Let's talk about what you are thinking" or "I hear that you are saying that you want a snack even though I am saying it is not a good time. What can you do to help yourself manage until it is lunchtime?" Sometimes the child acts toward someone else in a way that the parent finds problematic. In that situation, the parent could say something like, "I see that your brother acts in ways that you find annoying. How do you think you can respond without hurting him?" And remember that providing the child with choices (see below) helps children feel respected and valued.

Reflections

- *What does respect mean to you?*

- *How can you help yourself be respectful toward your child even while your child may be pushing your buttons?*

- *Can you envision a way of being respectful to your child that allows you to feel respectful toward yourself at the same time?*

BE PROACTIVE

Many parent–child conflicted situations can be prevented when parents behave in a proactive, as opposed to a reactive, manner. Much of children's misbehavior and conflict occur as a result of parents failing to think ahead and plan. This means anticipating your child's needs and planning accordingly. For example, you can anticipate that your child will get hungry or thirsty if you're going out on an excursion, so you can plan to have snacks and drinks available. Otherwise, your child may be uncomfortable and hence behave unpleasantly. Likewise, if you know that your child generally gets tired or cranky at a certain time of day, try not to plan something that will be too taxing for them. Older children may have their own plans, needs, or ideas about what they want to do when they're with you, and you can take that into account before your planning. You can check in with them regarding how much homework they have or whether they have any rehearsals or performances that they need to plan for or tests that they need to study for. If you can anticipate what their needs will be as much as possible, you can avoid miscommunications, misunderstandings, and mismatched expectations for your time together.

A second way to be proactive is to make sure that your expectations for your child are appropriate given their age and stage of development. For example, a proactive parent would not take a young child out for dinner at a fancy restaurant because behaving appropriately for that setting is probably beyond the young child's capacity. A proactive parent would not expect a very young child to share a new toy with a friend at a playdate, understanding that they are not developmentally at the place where they can share an exciting new toy. A proactive parent might discuss the situation with the child asking them if they want to share the toy or whether they would like to put it away during the playdate. Examples relevant for older children include not leaving a mischievous teenager home alone for several hours knowing that that might be expecting too much of the child. A parent of a tween might not let them have total control over their schedule knowing that they might not be able to juggle studying and homework with downtime. It might be asking too much of the child to let them have their cell phone in their room at night because it might be too tempting and beyond the child's capacity to manage their own impulses. Proactive parents know what is appropriate to expect of a child given the personality of the child and their developmental level and then act accordingly.

Another aspect of being proactive is to be clear with your child about what is expected of them when you go into a particular situation whether it's visiting a relative in the hospital, eating out for dinner, going on a playdate, or starting school. Any new situation can be challenging for a young child, and the more that you as a proactive parent can provide your child with some guidance about what is expected of them in that situation, the more likely it is that they will be able to behave in a way that works for you and for them. For example, if you're going on a playdate for the first time, you might want to practice with your child how to ask to share a toy (you can practice taking turns with them) or how to let you know if they need to use the bathroom since they wouldn't necessarily know where it is in an unfamiliar home visiting a friend (a proactive parent might also ask the child if they need to use the restroom since the child might forget to ask you until it is too late). With an older child, you could discuss what to expect if they are going to the mall with friends. You can clarify how often they need to check in with you, what to do if they get separated from their friends, what to do if a stranger approaches them, and other scenarios that it will be helpful to anticipate. Remember to allow your child to participate in the development of the rules and expectations so that they buy into them rather than having them imposed. The more information you can provide the child about what to expect in the new situation and what you expect of them, the less likely it will be that you will have misunderstandings.

Another aspect of being proactive is making sure to teach your child how to perform the various skills they will need to learn. For example, if you want your child to "clean their room," you need to explain to your child what that means to you. You need to show them how to make a bed, how to pick up their dirty clothes off the floor and put them in the hamper, how to dust the bookshelves, and anything else that goes into your definition of cleaning the room. If you want your child to get dressed by themselves, it would be unfair and demeaning to your child to simply say to them, "What's the matter with you? Why don't you know how to do that?" or "Go upstairs and get dressed and come down when you're ready." Your child may not know what that means. You need to show them how to put on their socks, how to put their pants on one leg at a time, how to put their shirt on over their head, and so on. The more you can teach your child in a warm and loving way how to do the things you want them to do, the less conflict and misbehavior you will have.

Reflections

- *What are some skills that your child is ready to learn now?*
- *What are some skills that you can practice with your child?*
- *Can you think of some basic expectations that you have for your child (be polite, be helpful)?*

ENGAGE IN REFLECTIVE PARENTING

Parents often react to their children in an impulsive or automatic fashion, especially if the child's behavior is undesirable, stressful, or embarrassing for the parent. This often results in parents doing or saying something that they might regret. If your child is already hurt, angry, rejecting, and distant, they may not be as forgiving as you would hope or want them to be if you do behave in a problematic way. Therefore, it is recommended that you engage in reflective parenting. In essence, this means that you slow down and try to think about what kind of parent you want to be and what you want your child to learn in any given situation—especially if they misbehave. If you can slow down and consider your parenting goals, you can choose to be more intentional in your parenting choices. You will be modeling for your child how to act in an intentional, instead of impulsive, manner. Examples of reflective parenting include not responding immediately to a problematic situation (unless your child is in danger or harming someone else). It means thinking about what your child needs in the situation, such as whether your child is tired, hungry, sick, afraid, or unclear about the expectations for the situation. Ask yourself whether your child has the skills and knowledge to do what you are asking. You want to make sure that you consider the situation from your child's perspective to see if that provides you with insight into their behavior. And you always want to consider how you want your child to experience you (remember, the goal is to be safe, loving, and available).

Reflections

- *How can you remember to pause before reacting to your child?*

- *What are your parenting goals? What are some characteristics and skills you want your child to have when they are a grown-up?*

- *Are there automatic parenting responses that you want to take out of rotation because they are not consistent with a positive parenting approach?*

USE EMOTION COACHING TO TEACH SELF-REGULATION

Emotion coaching is a communication strategy that helps children develop the capacity to understand and regulate their emotions (Gottman, 1998). When parents engage in emotion coaching, they are teaching their children how emotions work and how to recognize and express their feelings in a healthy manner. There are many benefits to emotion coaching. Parents who engage in emotion coaching have children who are less likely to become irrationally overaroused with negative emotions. These children can work through difficult times without behaving in a way that harms themselves or others.

Emotion coaching has many components, the first of which is talking about emotions. You as a parent can label emotions as you feel them, such as "Boy, I am feeling proud that I got that promotion!" or "That is so frustrating when someone cuts me off in the car." You can also label emotions that your child is feeling, such as

"I see that you are feeling very sad right now that your playdate ended." You can also talk about emotions that characters in books and movies might be feeling. The message that you want to convey is that it is OK to feel whatever you are feeling and that you as the parent accept the child's emotions. You never want to convey that it is not acceptable for your child to have a feeling, such as "Don't be sad, it's only a movie" or "That is so naughty of you to feel jealous of your brother." People really don't have control over their emotions, and you don't want to shame your child for feeling whatever it is that they are feeling. You want to convey acceptance of your child's feeling. For example, you can say, "I see that you are feeling angry at your brother for taking your toy. I don't like it when people take things away from me."

The second aspect of emotion coaching, after labeling emotions, is to model and teach how to manage emotions. That is, while your child will feel whatever they are feeling, how they manage their emotions really matters and is something that they can learn. Here is a perfect example of the intersection of warmth and high expectations. You can be very sympathetic about what the child is feeling and still convey clear expectations about what is and is not OK for the child to do in response to the feeling. The best way to do that is for the parent to demonstrate this in the moment. A parent might say, "I am so frustrated that the line is long. I am going to distract myself by singing a song," "I am worried about this problem at work. I am going to take some deep breaths to help me focus and prepare for the meeting," or "I am disappointed in my friend for not remembering my birthday. I think I will let her know that my feelings are hurt."

The final aspect is to intentionally teach your child these skills for emotion regulation. If your child is upset and expressing a negative emotion, you can ask them—with loving kindness—what they need to help them feel better or help resolve the situation. Sometimes your child just needs to know that you notice what they are feeling and care enough to check in with them. You might ask, "You were feeling a little sad earlier. How are you doing now?" And sometimes children need more concrete assistance in managing their emotions so that they can remain respectful to others—including the person they are feeling upset with. You might ask your child what they need to feel better or what would help them calm down so that they don't feel overwhelmed by such big emotions. You can teach your child breathing techniques to help calm their mind and body down. Remember that what you do to help your child deal with their emotions has to come from a place of love and respect rather than an effort to control, shame, or blame the child for what they are feeling.

Reflections
- *Are there certain emotions that you are less comfortable with in yourself and/or your child?*
- *What can you do to accept all emotions in yourself as well as in your child?*

BE ENCOURAGING

As noted elsewhere in this book, children need to feel the positive regard of their parents. One specific way to express that is through an attitude of encouragement, conveying to your child that you, their parent, believe in them and know that they are capable of learning and growing into a wonderful, competent person. Children behave better when they feel proud of their accomplishments and hopeful that they can do even better in the future. The point of encouragement is to help your child develop perseverance in the face of frustration and obstacles so that they don't give up in despair when things don't work out the way they want them to. Encouragement builds confidence and self-esteem in children, and children who feel happy with themselves are generally better behaved and easier to parent.

Some specific aspects of encouragement include noticing when the child is feeling proud of themselves and commenting on their internal sense of satisfaction. You might say to your child, "You seem so proud of yourself for pulling your grade up." This creates a feeling of closeness and connection and also involves some emotion coaching because you are labeling the child's feeling. Make sure to focus on the *effort* not the outcome. "I see you working hard to build that tower. That is what I call stick-to-it-ive-ness!" rather than "What a great tower you built."

Another aspect of being encouraging is to focus on learning as a process rather than an outcome. If your child is trying to accomplish something and it is not going well, you can offer supportive statements such as "What a good start. Next time it will probably go even better" or "You are playing that piano piece better each time." You could even share something that it took you a while to get the hang of and how glad you are that you stuck with it. And of course, you can be empathic with how frustrating it feels when things don't work out exactly how we wanted them to.

Showing interest in your child's process and efforts also keeps the focus away from just an outcome. For example, if the child is drawing a picture, instead of saying that it is a "good" or "nice" picture, you can invite your child to tell you about the picture, what parts came out the way they had hoped, and what parts they want to keep working on. Likewise, you can ask your child which types of math problems they enjoy or what led them to choose a particular sport or instrument.

Make sure to convey to your child that mistakes are opportunities to learn as opposed to expressions of defeat and failure. If your child doesn't achieve the grade that they were hoping for on a test, you can go over the problems together to see what they need to work on some more. You want to convey that there is usually a way to learn something from a mistake that will help them do better next time. You want to avoid shaming the child for making a mistake because then they may decide it is not worth trying to do new and challenging things. Of course, you can convey an attitude of positivity when you share with your child the challenges you have faced and what you learned from them. Children who feel hopeful about their ability to do well generally are happier and easier to parent.

Reflections

- *How can you remember to be kind to yourself and your child when success does not come immediately or readily?*

- *What are some examples of a time when you felt encouraged to persevere?*

- *What are some areas where your child needs to feel more encouragement?*

INVITE COOPERATION

Reducing child misbehavior—increasing cooperation—is an important goal of positive parenting. The more that you and your child are on the same page, the better off you will be. There are several techniques for increasing your child's cooperation with you.

Polite Requests

Most people, including if not especially children, would prefer to be asked, rather than commanded, to do something. This is often especially true of a hurt, angry, rejecting, distant child who is predisposed to experience you as uncaring. Thus, make sure not to make too many commands or demands of your child. They will most likely respond better to a polite request such as "Please help me set the table." And if you add a "thank you" to the end—even before the child even does it, that really boosts cooperation. Once your child does the task, make sure to throw in another expression of appreciation. When children feel appreciated and noticed for their helpfulness, they want to be more helpful. You could even express your desire for their help as a statement rather than a request such as "I would love to have a hand setting the table" or "I could use your help right now."

Offer Choices

When possible, provide your child with choices to help them feel a sense of agency and purpose. These opportunities to make choices help children feel that you trust them, boosting their sense of closeness with you. Make sure that when you give your child opportunities to choose that you provide a limited set of options and that you are okay with either option the child might select. In other words, don't ask your child if they want to take a bath or do their homework unless you are prepared for them to not take a bath or not do their homework. Examples of options might be "Do you want to wear your red shirt or your blue shirt today?" or "Do you want an apple or a banana for your snack?" One goal of parenting is to raise a child who can make good choices for themselves, and it is never too early to provide your child with opportunities to experience the pleasure of making choices. Children are much more likely to be cooperative if they are provided with opportunities to experience self-direction and agency. Rather than arguing with your child about why they need to take a bath, you are exciting your child with the options of hopping to the bath like a bunny rabbit or flying like an airplane. For a school-age child, options might include deciding which playground to go to, which friend to invite over for a playdate, or whether to come to the supermarket or stay home. For much older children, choices might be which club to join in school, whether to do homework before or after a playdate, and how short to cut their hair. The more children take responsibility for their own choices, the less inclined your child will be to blame you for being too controlling or for making a bad choice in the event that the child is disappointed in the outcome.

When–Then

It often happens that children want to do something, and the parent does not think that the time is right. A child might want a playdate or to go to the store or play outside or have screen time while the parent has an expectation that something else should be happening such as a chore or homework. Rather than saying no to the child or becoming annoyed with their requests, you can say, "When X is done, then you can do Y." As an alternative you can say you can do Y as soon as X is done. It is important for you to convey to your child that you are on their side and always want to give them what they want. This strategy increases your child's cooperation because they will feel that you love them and want them to have pleasure and satisfaction. You are providing them with a way to get what they want without your reprimanding or shaming them for not yet doing the chore or homework or whatever it is that needs to get done first. When–then can also work when you need to do something before you are available. If your child asks you to take them to the store, you can say, "When I am done folding laundry, then I will be free to take you to the store. If you would like to assist me, the laundry will get done sooner." That might entice the child to volunteer to assist you with the task. If they choose to do so, make sure to express appreciation.

Family Meetings

Another way to invite cooperation is to hold family meetings to discuss schedules, plans, concerns, expectations, and anything else that will help each member of the family to feel a sense of belonging and being cared about. You can have family members take turns running the meeting to foster a feeling of shared purpose and shared agency. Of course, the parent is the ultimate decision maker when it comes to issues related to safety and embodying family values, but many smaller decisions can be discussed and decided as a team. The more the child is a part of the decision-making process, the less they will have to complain about and the less likely someone else will be able to undermine the jointly arrived at decisions.

Use Positive Discipline Strategies

Even if you follow all the advice in this book, there will be times when your child misbehaves or is uncooperative, which may require some form of response from you. This is especially true if your child is already hurt, angry, rejecting, and distant. No child follows all the rules and lives up to all expectations. That is simply unrealistic to expect of your child. The question for you as the parent is how you want to respond when your child requires feedback about their behavior. The first point—and it is an important one—is that there is a difference between discipline and punishment. The word *discipline* derives from the Latin word meaning *disciple*, to teach. You can think of discipline as having the intention to teach your child to help them to be their best self. Punishment, on the other hand, is essentially designed to make the child feel bad in the moment. The premise is if the child suffers because of their bad behavior, they will not engage in that bad behavior again. And sometimes punishment is also designed to provide the parent with gratification by releasing their hostility toward their child when they are misbehaving. It is an essential component of positive parenting that children do not have to be made to feel bad to improve their behavior. That does not mean that it is a free-for-all and that children can behave however they want, whenever they want. It is your job as the parent to socialize your child and to teach them how to get along with others; how to be helpful, polite, respectful, and cooperative; and how to be a self-sufficient, functioning, competent adult. And that can be achieved with a variety of discipline strategies, none of which involve punishing or causing pain to the child.

Ignoring Minor Irritating Behaviors
The first discipline strategy involves simply ignoring the child when the child is engaging in undesirable behavior for the purpose of getting your attention. An example might be potty talk from a toddler or swearing from a tween. If the child is not in danger of harming themselves or someone else, the parent can simply go about their business, not reprimanding their child nor providing positive feedback in the form of smiling, winking, nodding, and so on. A particularly damaging type of rewarding the child involves creating a video of the moment and then posting it on social media. Most likely the child will understand that the parent thinks it is amusing and "post worthy." If the parent takes pleasure in the child's "naughty" behavior in any visible way, that will reinforce the behavior.

If the parent is going to ignore minor behavior, it does not need to be done with harshness and cruelty. There's no need for the parent to say anything negative or derogatory toward the child. In fact, the principle of ignoring minor irritating behaviors is to be neutral and simply go about your business, and the child may soon stop the annoying behavior because they are getting somewhat less parental attention. The child may consciously or unconsciously "get the message" without any appreciable upset. And then they will feel the pleasure of the positive attention from the parent, and their need to be "naughty" will be diminished.

Distraction and Redirection
Distraction and redirection are highly effective discipline strategies, especially for younger children. What they involve is drawing the child's attention away from the behavior that the parent does not want the child to engage in and redirecting their attention to something that is more desirable from the parent's point of view. For example, if a toddler is reaching on the shelf for something that the parent does not want the child to touch, the parent can simply say "Can you find the doggy in this picture?" and thereby

draw the child's attention away from the object on the shelf and direct their attention to the book. It doesn't have to be new to the child; it is just new in that moment. Redirection is a more explicit version of distraction because it involves informing the child that what they're doing and how they're doing it needs to be modified. For example, a parent might remind the child that the couch isn't for jumping on, but the child can jump on the trampoline in the backyard and invite the child to do that instead. There is a clear message to the child that what they are doing is not working for the parent, and a suggestion is made for how to modify their behavior to meet everyone's needs.

Time-In

Sometimes children—especially younger children—become emotionally dysregulated. This means that they become flooded with negative emotion, usually frustration. This happens when children can't get what they want or are overwhelmed with the demands of the situation. When that happens, they may engage in what is typically referred to as a meltdown or a temper tantrum. Some parenting experts make a distinction between a meltdown and a temper tantrum, with the former being a more involuntary flooding of emotion that overwhelms the child to the point that they simply cannot function in that moment. A temper tantrum, on the other hand, is usually more intentional on the part of the child as a behavior strategy designed to change the parent's mind about something. A classic example would be the child who wants the parent to buy them candy in the checkout line at the supermarket and the parent says no. In response, the child throws themselves on the floor screaming, crying, pounding their fists on the floor, and refusing to be cooperative. Sometimes it's hard to tell the difference between a meltdown and a temper tantrum. Either way, the positive parenting approach does not endorse time-out as a parenting strategy, especially for children who are having a meltdown or a tantrum. Many positive parenting experts today recommend that the parent stay near their child, making empathic and/or sympathetic comments such as "This is so hard for you right now" and allowing the child to feel their feelings without judgment, recriminations, or negative attributions that the child is being bad or naughty. In these situations, a time-in would involve the parents staying near the child and being nurturing and sympathetic without giving the child what the child is demanding and perhaps when the child is ready, snuggling with the child and helping them regain their equilibrium. The problem with time-out from a positive parenting perspective is that it involves banishing the child when they are already having a difficult time coping. The message can be received by the child that they are acceptable only when they are behaving how you want them to behave. And if they are having a hard time, they need to go away and collect themselves all by themselves and then they can come back when they are feeling or behaving better. All the hard work of managing the emotional upheaval is something the child is expected to do on their own. Positive parenting experts believe that it is better to stay near the child and comfort them, functioning as a coregulator. In this way, when the child is overwhelmed, the parent sort of takes over the wheel and lets the child ride through their emotional upheaval knowing that the parent is nearby and available, nurturing and caring. It might even be advised to have a space in the home referred to as the time-in space. This could be a warm and friendly space. You can name the spot such as "our special spot" or "the cuddle corner." You and your child can decorate this space with some pillows, a stuffed animal, a book, and other comforting items. If you notice your child beginning to become dysregulated, you can say to your child that it looks like they are having a hard time right now and maybe it is a good time to go to the cuddle corner and spend a couple of minutes together. Some might fear that a time-in reinforces negative behavior. Some might think that a child will misbehave to get to go to the cuddle corner. But that's not actually the way it works. If children have their emotional needs met enough of the time, they will not misbehave to get cuddled and nurtured. They will know that they can always ask for cuddles if they need them and the parent will be affectionate throughout the day so the child would not need to misbehave to get affection from the parent. Children who receive enough love, attention, and affection are generally more cooperative and better behaved, not worse.

Natural Consequences

Even though positive parenting generally avoids punishments and other punitive parenting strategies, that does not mean that children never experience the consequences of their misbehavior. There are plenty of times when the child misbehaves and the parents can let nature take its course to teach the child a lesson. For example, if a child does not want to bring a sweater or coat with them after the parent has reminded them or invited them to, the child might experience the inconvenience of being cold that naturally occurs because they made the choice to not bring a sweater or a coat. The parent does not need to rub the child's nose in their mistake. If the parent says "I told you to bring a coat and you didn't listen to me; now it's just too bad that you're cold," the child will feel ashamed and resentful and probably will not learn the lesson that you want to teach your child. The lesson you want to teach is that sometimes when a parent recommends you bring a coat, you should probably bring a coat. And that is a lesson that your child can learn through the natural consequence of being cold if they chose to not bring their coat. There is no need to get into a power struggle with the child about whether they are going to put on their coat. You can let the child decide and then deal with the consequences; just make sure not to humiliate the child for making a choice that didn't work out. We all make choices that don't have great consequences for us, and there's no need to be humiliated. We can learn the lesson without the shame.

There are times when the consequence would be so dire or dramatic that the parent cannot let the child learn from their own actions/consequences. For example, the parent cannot let the child touch a hot stove, run out into the street, or hurt somebody else. Those are times when the parent must step in and use one of the other strategies such as redirecting the child or explaining what the expectations are in advance so the child doesn't do that or being proactive and holding the child's hand while you're outside until the child is old enough to play safely without having to hold the parent's hand. Natural consequences are only for when the consequence would be a deterrent but not cause harm to the child.

It is important to distinguish between natural consequences and logical consequences. Many parenting experts still promote a discipline strategy referred to as logical consequences although the field of positive parenting is moving away from logical consequences. That is because it is really just another form of punishment. The premise of a logical consequence is that the parent imposes a consequence on the child as opposed to the consequence happening naturally to teach a child not to do something. For example, the child doesn't put their cell phone down when they're supposed to, so the parent imposes the consequence of the cell phone being taken away; the child doesn't go to bed on time, so they must go to bed earlier the next day; or the child didn't clean up their room, so their toys are taken away from them. The parent imposes a consequence as opposed to a consequence happening naturally. It is referred to as logical because ideally the imposed consequence logically relates to the misbehavior. The intention of a logical consequence is to teach the child that if they do not do what the parent wants them to do, they will suffer a consequence imposed by the parent. It is designed to be a deterrent to the child. The problem with logical consequences is that they involve the parent imposing some form of pain on the child to teach the child to do better. Although a logical consequence is preferable to purposefully humiliating the child, screaming at the child, or hitting the child, it is not the preferred positive parenting discipline strategy because it can be harsh and thus engender a feeling of resentment in the child.

Mutual Problem Solving

Mutual problem solving helps when a child misbehaves and the parent works with the child to discuss what happened and what can be done so that it does not happen again. It is called *mutual* problem solving because the parent and child engage in a mutually respectful, open conversation as opposed to the parent imposing their understanding of what happened onto the child and then deciding what should happen in response. It is referred to as problem solving because the goal is to prevent the problem from happening again and determining whether there is a solution that needs to be implemented to remedy the situation. As an example, if your child failed a math test, you could have a conversation with your child about what's going on with math. Rather than punishing the child (as some parents automatically or reflexively do) when their child does not get a good grade, such as taking away their cell phone, the purpose of mutual problem solving is to understand first and foremost why the child failed their math test. Perhaps the child needs glasses because they can't see the blackboard, the teacher is unnecessarily harsh, the child needs a tutor, or the child is being bullied in class or in school. The first element of mutual problem solving is to look at why the problem happened in the first place. The second part of mutual problem solving is determining what needs to be done.

As another example, if your child were playing ball in the house and broke a window, mutual problem solving might involve a discussion of expectations of where ball playing can occur and about how the window will get repaired. Possible solutions could include the child having a bake sale or babysitting to make money to pay for the repaired window. Perhaps the child has an allowance or has saved money, which can be used to pay for the window, or the child can do extra chores around the house to make up for the fact that you will have to spend time and money repairing the window. The principle here is that if children participate in a mutually respectful conversation about what happened and how to remedy the situation and all of this is done without shame, blame, recriminations, or humiliation, the child will learn how to do better and will understand that reparations are possible. If you simply punish your child for their "bad behavior," they might not learn all of these really important lessons and might end up feeling misunderstood and resentful for being punished (and will someday have to unlearn the idea that they are bad, stupid, and shameful).

A Word about Spanking

Another discipline strategy that is strongly discouraged in the positive parenting literature is any form of physical punishment of children, including spanking, hitting, pinching, swatting, popping, whooping, and the like. All forms of physical pain imposed on a child to teach them a lesson is a highly problematic parenting strategy that is strongly discouraged by leading experts (https://www.endphysicalpunishment.org/). The research literature is very comprehensive at this point. There are over one thousand studies that were conducted across the world demonstrating that physical punishment is harmful to children and that it is ineffective in achieving most of its intended goals. It is harmful in that parents can lose control and end up physically abusing their children even when their intention was simply to teach the child a lesson about their misbehavior. More than one third of physical abuse incidents start off as some form of physical punishment that gets out of hand. In addition, the research shows that corporal punishment is ineffective (Gershoff et al., 2018). It does not reduce child misbehavior in the long run, although it can function as an immediate deterrent for children to stop their misbehavior. In fact, over time, spanking increases child aggression and misbehavior.

Conclusion

In Part I, four aspects of in-person communicating with your hurt, angry, rejecting, distant child have been presented (i.e., enhance the attachment, don't take the bait, foster four values, and be a positive parent). These strategies work together to help you be the best parent you can be to increase the warmth and love shared between you and your child and to help decrease incentives for your child to feel justified in their negative stance toward you. You also most likely have opportunities to communicate with your child during periods of separation. Refining the quantity and quality of messages you send to your child also has enormous potential to both enhance the relationship and reduce the hurt, anger, rejection, and distance that your child is feeling from you and expressing toward you.

Part II

How to Communicate by Text Message with a Hurt, Angry, Rejecting, Distant Child

In this part of the book, we will explain how to communicate by text with a hurt, angry, rejecting, and distant (HARD) child. Whatever the cause of your child's negative feelings toward you, it is essential that you find ways to communicate that represent yourself as a safe, loving, and available parent. Part II offers the following sections: (1) how and why to send text messages, (2) basic messaging techniques, (3) messaging tips and considerations, (4) thirty types of text messages and things to consider for each type, and (5) responding to the responses.

How and Why to Text with a Child

IF YOU HAVE A CHILD OLD ENOUGH TO HAVE A SMARTPHONE, communication is probably primarily by text messages. That is just the reality of modern technology and communication. If you want to communicate with your child, you need to know how to send messages. Part II of the book will provide you with 370 ideas for how to communicate by text message with a child with whom you have a conflicted or distant relationship. It is possible that you still have an ongoing in-person relationship with this child and are sending messages during periodic separations. It is also possible that you don't have any ongoing contact. This portion of the book is relevant for any hurt, angry, rejecting, distant child who is old enough to have a device that receives messages.

Because the relationship is distant and/or conflicted, it is likely that you will struggle with not just whether you should send a message (more on that below) but also with what you should say. This part of the book is designed to give you many ideas about the "what" to provide you with a wider choice of options than you might be aware of. Please note that throughout this book, the term "child" is used to refer to someone you are a parent of regardless of their age. Here, we refer to a "child" as being someone who is old enough to receive messages on a phone. Also, please note that to continue to be gender neutral, the pronoun "they" will be used even when referring to a singular child.

Our goal is to make it as easy as possible for you to send messages to your child and remove the barrier of "I don't know what to say." We know that it is painful to continue to reach out to a child who never or rarely responds back. The string of your own messages on the right side of your smartphone screen—with little if any response texts on the left side of the screen—can feel demoralizing and create a sense of futility. That sadness and sense of hopelessness can impede creativity and sap you of energy—the energy that is needed to keep forging ahead. Our goal is to give you many ideas for those days when the ideas just don't come and all you can think of to write is the same old same old. You can turn to this part of the book when the well runs dry so that even on those darkest and most painful days, you can continue to reach out to your child. Please do not feel that the options provided in the book are the only choices you have. You may have your own ideas and—if they are consistent with the dos and don'ts below—we encourage you to use them as well.

Reflections

- *What are some words that come to mind when you think about reaching out to your child?*

- *Do you notice that they are primarily positive, primarily negative, or mixed?*

- *What are some other things that you have done in your life that were as hard then as messaging your child is right now?*

- *Would it be helpful to remind yourself that you are always a parent even when your child is hurt, angry, and rejecting you?*

- *Can you hold in your heart the value that you have to your child?*

Why You Should Message Your Child Even Though You May Not Get a Response

The short answer is that even though you and your child have conflict and/or distance in your relationship, you are the parent, the role model of responsibility, hope, and acceptance in human relationships. Therefore, you need to make the greater effort in maintaining the relationship. By continuing to send messages, you are showing your child—through your words—that you value the relationship, you have love in your heart, and there is always hope for improvement and meaningful connection. Through your life experience, you have probably come to learn that sometimes people have distance and conflict in their relationships but that they can find a way to work things out that feels right for everyone. This is a message that is important for you to convey to your child, and the best way to do that is for you to live that ideal by reaching out despite the current problems in the relationship.

Will one message make a difference? Most likely, the answer is no. Generally, no one message is going to turn things around. It may be helpful to think of each message as a grain of sand that you put on one side of the scale. No one grain of sand is going to tip things in your favor (unless it is that final one after the weight of enough has already been amassed). No one grain of sand can make a difference (by itself) just like no one grain of sand can create a beach. But the accumulation of all your messages—like the accumulation of grains of sand on a beach—can create something beautiful and powerful. Taken together, the weight (or force of love) of your messages—your ongoing and consistent message to your child that you love them, are thinking about them, are holding them close in your heart—can create a receptivity in your child's heart. At the very least, you are not reinforcing to your child that you don't care and have given up so that you can't even bother to text. Remember, you can never know or be able to predict how many messages or which message will spark a response from your child. If you knew exactly what message would work for which child, you wouldn't need a book with hundreds of possible messages. There are probably just too many factors at play including everything else that is going on in your child's life and in their heart and mind. From earlier research, we have learned that there are many catalysts to a rejecting child coming back to their rejected parent (Baker, 2007). There were many possible sparks to ignite the thought "Gee, maybe that parent isn't all bad. Maybe there is value in that relationship." And that was before text messaging even existed. We know from our current work with parents with a hurt, angry, rejecting, distant child that the continued reaching out does make a difference. Sometimes the child will say to the formerly cutoff parent "You know all of those messages you sent? Well, I was actually reading them even though I never responded." It is with this understanding that we encourage you and urge you to continue to reach out to your child, especially via text messaging as one meaningful way to show your love and to carry the torch to lead the way toward the light and life of a closer relationship.

Another image that may be helpful is that of the mother bunny in the beloved baby book *The Runaway Bunny*. In this book, the baby bunny imagines various scenarios of running away. Perhaps he will join the circus or become a crocus in a hidden flower garden, a bird that flies away, a boat that sails away, or a little boy that runs into a house. In response, the mother never appears to get her feelings hurt or to get angry. She always responds with a loving message such as "If you become a bird and fly away from me, I will become a tree that you come home to"; "If you become a crocus in a hidden garden, then I will become a gardener and I will find you"; "If you join the circus and become a trapeze artist, I will become a tightrope walker and I will walk across the air to you"; or "If you become a little boy and run into a house, I will become a mother and catch you in my arms and hug you." In the end, the little bunny decides he might as well be her little bunny. This mother has the right idea. She never feels

offended or insulted by her child's desire for separation and independence. She maintains an unwavering positive image of her role
in her child's life and is able to respond to his rejection in a loving
and connected manner. To be fair, in the book there doesn't seem
to be a third party undermining her, and for sure, it is easier for
that parent to stay compassionate and connected. But still, what
a role model of a parent in a challenging parent–child situation
and a useful image of the attitude that is required of you when
thinking about sending messages.

An anecdote from a former alienated child might be useful here. She was interviewed for an earlier book, years after
her alienation experience, in which her mother and stepfather
prevented her from having a relationship with her father. She
shared that her father came to visit every Sunday. Every Sunday,
he would drive over to the mother's house, park his car at the
curb, and walk up to and knock on the front door. Every Sunday, the mother, stepfather, this woman, and her siblings would
stand inside the house on the other side of the door. They never
answered the door, and this woman never had an opportunity to
see her father. In fact, she and her siblings would yell through the
door "Go away!" and that they did not want to see him and they
were not going to come out. Eventually, according to this woman,
her father stopped coming. And it is easy to imagine why. From
his point of view, there was no point. Why should he drive over
there and get his hopes up thinking that perhaps he'll see his
children? Why should he walk up to the house and knock on
the door only to be rejected and become dejected and thoroughly
disappointed once again? From his point of view, the visit was a
failure. All he got to do was knock on the door. When she was
asked what it was like for her when her father stopped knocking
on the door and trying to see his children, she explained that she
was shocked. She never expected that her rejection of him would
result in his deciding to stop trying to see her. She explained that
from her experience, the knock was the whole point of the visit.

She knew she was not going to be allowed out. There was no way her mother and stepfather would let her see her father. From her point of view, the knock was everything because it represented her father's ongoing love for her. The knock was the message just like your message is that you have not given up.

Sometimes children think (or have been told) that it is okay to cut people off. They may be getting this message from their other parent, their friends, a coach, a spouse, a therapist, or even from professionals in books and videos. You may be the only person in your child's life who is conveying the message that the relationship has meaning and value despite its problems, that the relationship is worth fighting for. If you don't reach out, then your child might not be getting that lesson from anyone. You are the torchbearer for the relationship and perhaps your child's future relationships with significant others. If you cannot or will not carry the torch, who will?

Reflections

- *Can you imagine that your child feels relieved to receive messages even if they are hurt and angry with you?*

- *Have you ever had the experience of telling someone you are hurt and angry with them and being disappointed that they did not pursue you?*

- *Is it helpful to imagine a beautiful beach with so many grains of sand, each of which contains a loving message from you to your child?*

- *Can you tap into your inner "runaway bunny" parent as you hold in your heart the value of the relationship even as your child is rejecting you?*

WHY YOU SHOULD ADD VARIETY TO YOUR MESSAGING

You may be wondering why you should go through all this effort of varying the message, wording, images, and so forth. Why not just send "I love you" every time? The thinking in support of variety is that you don't want your children to habituate to the same message every day. It will become dull, extraneous . . . invisible. Variety may cause them to take notice in a way that they might not otherwise. The second reason to try different messages (i.e., content, wording, and visuals) is because you probably cannot know which ones will be most impactful. In addition, it will possibly register for your children that you are putting a lot of effort and thought into the messages you send and *that* alone is a message that you value the relationship. Also, some of the suggestions are mostly or purely visual, which can allow you to speak directly to your child's heart from your heart. A brief image of a bunny leaping in the air is sure to warm even the most cynical child's heart and bring a smile to their face, even if just for a moment.

Reflections
- *How can you tap into your creativity and capacity for showing affection to send a variety of messages to your child?*
- *In what ways would it be easier for you to have variety in your messages to your child?*
- *In what ways would it be harder?*

Basic Messaging Techniques

A TEXT MESSAGE IS A WORD OR VISUAL MESSAGE CREATED FROM one cell phone and sent to another cell phone. The mechanics of sending a message are different depending on whether you are using a smartphone or another type of phone. Regardless of the type of phone, there is a process for accessing your contacts and/or typing in a recipient's phone number in order to send a message.

TEXT

At its most basic, a message comprises words such as "I love you," which appear exactly as you type them. When sending messages, many people shorten words, for example, typing "luv" instead of "love" or "U" instead of "you," and this can add variety to your texting and keep things novel and interesting. However, words are just the beginning of the messaging world. Smartphones and some flip phones have additional options for customizing messages, which are described below.

EMOJIS

Once you click on the message box, you should see a smiling face icon at the bottom of your screen; if you click on that, you can enter the world of emojis. Emojis are instantly recognizable cartoon-like pictures, which can be used as substitutions for words in a text, such as a picture of a heart instead of the word "love" or a picture of a snowflake instead of the word "snow." Using emojis adds an element of novelty and creativity to your messages. Instead of typing out "I love you," you could use an eyeball, a heart, and a ewe. Emojis multiply the number of ways you can convey the same idea.

MEMOJIS

A memoji is an emoji that you create to resemble you. You can then import this memoji into a message in various poses (e.g., waving, sending love, or with a heart or peace sign). To create a memoji, you tap on the memoji option on the option strip under the message box (it looks like a person with hearts in their eyes). From there, you can select the shape of the face, skin color, hair color, color of eyes and brows, and so on to create a character that looks something like you. You can also use an existing memoji of an animal (e.g., rabbit or giraffe).

IMAGES

You will also notice another icon next to the message box that looks like the letter "A"; if you click on that, you will see a menu of options below the message box. One of the options is a red circle with a magnifying glass in it with the word "images" under it. If you click on that, you can enter a much larger set of visual options in addition to emojis that are available to be inserted into a message. You can search for "love" in the image search bar, for example, and find animated images of people saying I love you, animals snuggling, teddy bears blowing kisses, and hundreds of other options to signal warmth and affection. If you search for images for "snow," you will find panda bears sliding in the snow, Charlie Brown licking a snowflake, people shoveling their cars out of snow, Bambi experiencing snow, a kitten playing in the snow, famous characters from movies enjoying the snow, and hundreds of other options. If you search images for "congratulations," you will find applauding sheep; President Biden saying "Congratulations, man"; Minions cheering; or Simon Cowell saying "Brilliant, well done." There are hundreds of options.

PHOTOGRAPHS

You will also notice that on the left side of the message bar is an icon of a camera; if you click on that, you can either take a picture to include in your message or select a picture from your camera roll that you have already taken. Likewise, you can create or select an existing video to send, perhaps of yourself speaking to your child, a stunning vista, or an object that you think will be of interest to them.

LINKS

You can paste a link from a website into the message box and send that to your child as well, and when your child clicks on the link, they will be taken to the website you selected. It could be to a music video, a news story, a recipe, a movie review, or any other item on the internet that you think would be of interest to your child.

Reflections

- *Do you feel comfortable learning new messaging techniques?*
- *What animal memoji would your child most like to see?*
- *Is there anything about messaging techniques that are uncomfortable for you?*
- *What do you need to feel ready to start messaging your child on a regular basis?*

CHAPTER SEVEN

Messaging Tips and Considerations

MESSAGE WITH LOVE—NOT RESENTMENT— IN YOUR HEART

WHATEVER MESSAGE YOU SEND, IT MUST BE SENT WITH LOVE IN your heart for your child. If you are feeling angry, resentful, or bitter, you should probably wait until you are in a more loving frame of mind before you hit send. There is nothing to be gained by texting an angry, frightening, or hurtful message, and you can bet that if you do, it will be used as proof that you are as bad as they (the cutting off individual and their supporters) say you are.

It is essential that all your communications show you to be safe, loving, and available. If your child is rejecting you because they have been manipulated by someone else, it has worked because your child has been convinced that you don't really love them, you are dangerous, and you have not really prioritized them. You must avoid doing anything that reinforces this false idea.

Examples of angry, frightening, hurtful texts would include anything insulting about the child or their other parent such as "You are as toxic as your mother"; "If you want to be a better person than your father, you will answer me"; or "Don't you see that your mother is manipulating you?" Also, avoid any threats to abandon your child such as "If you cannot bother to return my texts, why should I keep writing you?" or "Perhaps I should do to you what you are doing to me and stop communicating." Any threat to stop communicating puts you in a bad or negative light because it makes you look mean and petty.

Reflections

- *Are you aware of when you feel resentment or anger toward your child before you express it to them?*
- *What happens inside your body when you feel resentment or anger?*
- *What do you need to do to ensure that you don't send an angry or resentful message?*
- *With whom can you share your feelings of anger and resentment so that you are not alone with those feelings?*

MESSAGE FROM A PLACE OF LOVE, NOT DESPERATION

Sometimes a strong feeling of love and desire for connection with a hurt, angry, rejecting, distant child can result in a feeling of desperation, which can unfortunately come across as scary or too intense for the child. Examples of texts to avoid include ones like the following: "Don't you know how much I miss you and yearn to be with you?"; "If only you knew how much I ache to be with you. You are on my mind morning, noon, and night"; and "I haven't been happy since the last time we were together. You are my whole life. Why won't you see me?" These kinds of messages can be burdensome to the child, who does not want to feel responsible for the parent's well-being. And too, they can come across as manipulative and guilt inducing.

Reflections

- *Are there times when you are more likely to feel desperate than other times?*

- *What happens inside your body and mind when you feel desperate for your child to respond to you and to reconnect in a meaningful way?*

- *What can you do and say to yourself so that you don't feel over-whelmed with grief and longing?*

- *Would it help to remind yourself that you are strong and capable and can handle whatever sad feelings you are having?*

- *Would it help to remind yourself that many parents are able to repair a relationship with their child and that once the relationship is restored, the memory of the painful separation will recede and fade?*

FOCUS ON THE POSITIVE

The purpose of messaging is to keep a feeling of closeness alive in the relationship and hopefully, to entice the child to feel less hurt, angry, rejecting, and distant. If your messages focus on the negative (e.g., of your life, your feelings, or scary things going on in the world), then your child may come to dread your messages and be even less likely to let go of some of the hurt, anger, rejection, and distance. However, if you know that something bad has happened to the child, you should acknowledge that to show that you care. Likewise, if you are aware that something bad has happened to someone important to the child, don't ignore that because it could seem callous given the child's positive feelings for that person.

Reflections

- *Can you remind yourself to read the messages before you send them and consider whether you are being too negative?*

- *Can you read your draft message and try to imagine how it would feel for your child to receive it?*

- *Is there someone you can call upon to give you feedback about your draft messages?*

Make Genuine and Clear Offers

Some of the suggested messages include offers to buy the child something or to give the child something that someone gave to you to pass on to them (e.g., a birthday gift that a relative asked you to give to them). Make sure that when you do, you don't imply or state that there are strings attached unless you very clearly have thought that through and decided you want to do that. For example, if you offer to buy or give your child something and the child accepts the offer, it is not appropriate to then add that they must come to your home and have a meal with you to receive the item. If you want something in return or an obligation is attached to an offer, you really need to be clear about it in the original message; otherwise, you will create the impression that you are not trustworthy. Sometimes it is appropriate to attach a condition to the item you are offering, but before you do, make sure you have considered the situation from all sides. In some situations, the basic complaint about a parent is something like "Everything you do is conditional. You never just give from your heart." In that case, it would be unwise to attach anything resembling a condition to an offer.

Reflections
- *How would it feel for you to make an offer to your child with no strings attached?*
- *How can you resist the temptation to use leverage in a way that will feel coercive to the child?*
- *How can your communication embody mutuality and connection without being transactional or conditional?*

Be Age Appropriate

Your children are continuing to grow and mature even if you are not currently in contact, and it may be hard for you to bear this in mind. A young child might enjoy a message saying "Snow!" with a snowflake emoji or an image of Winnie the Pooh dancing in the snow, but a tween might find that painfully embarrassing or uncomfortable. Remember how old your child is now, instead of thinking about them as they were when you were last with them.

Reflections

- *How has your child grown and changed since you last had meaningful contact?*

- *How can you mourn the lost time with your child while still accepting them for who they are now?*

BE RESPECTFUL OF ALL PEOPLE

Much content online is not appropriate for your child because it is sexist, ageist, racist, biased, and/or violent; be sure that all words and images are devoid of any content that is offensive or insulting to your child, their friends, and their general sensibility. The world is rapidly changing in terms of an increasing awareness of exploitation of people from other cultures, races, ethnicities, sexual orientations, genders, and so forth. Make sure that you are up to date in your awareness of these issues so that assumptions and "isms" don't creep into your messaging.

Reflections

- *Are there aspects of your child's identity that you are not as comfortable with as your child would like you to be?*

- *Do you feel that your child's identity is authentic or imposed/manipulated by someone else?*

- *If you sense inauthenticity, can you refrain from conveying that to your child?*

- *Would it be helpful to remember that sometimes children experiment with different identities and that it doesn't mean that the changes are set in stone?*

AVOID HOT BUTTON ISSUES

Society is increasingly polarized around politics, cultural issues, and even science and technology. Ideally, your messages will not reference issues your child feels strongly about and that the two of you don't agree on. For example, if you and your child do not see eye-to-eye on gender issues, religion, vaccinations, or political affiliations, it is probably best to avoid any mention of them in your messages. If you believe in a different religion or political ideology, do not send them a tract or article from the internet to convert or "enlighten" them. This will unnecessarily antagonize your child and lead them to feel that you don't really care about them and that you just have an agenda to prove them wrong or win an argument. There is a time and place to discuss these issues, but such a message sent to a hurt, angry, rejecting, distant child is counterproductive. The only exception would be if your child brings up the topic; in that case, your response should be to thank the child for asking your opinion or sharing theirs and then to try to find common ground.

Reflections

- *Are there issues that you know you should avoid because they are likely to enflame a negative feeling between you?*

- *How can you demonstrate your interest in your child's views (should your child choose to raise the issues with you) even if you don't think that you will agree with them?*

- *Can you hold on to the idea that your child is developing and that ideas that are held dear today may not be in the future?*

DO NOT EMBARRASS YOUR CHILD

You want to take extreme care when messaging your child that you do not do anything that could embarrass them. This could involve pictures of them as a naked baby, an unflattering photo (e.g., chubby, in a wet diaper, or picking their nose), or a clip of their singing off-key or performing poorly at something. Messages could also be embarrassing if you refer to your child with a babyish nickname or share a memory of something that the child considers shameful and private.

Even though your intention is to show your child being delightful, they might feel upset with you for putting that information in a message. It is established at this point that anything sent via the internet can never be deleted permanently (even if you delete the message). Someone else could have seen the message you sent and snapped a picture of it, someone could access your child's phone and forward the message, or someone could have seen it and told others about it. Youth—especially tweens and teens—can be susceptible to feeling shame if they are deemed to be uncool, babyish, or unattractive. It is best not to do anything that will cause your child to feel bad about themselves or could be used against them by peers who want to bully or shame them. That would exacerbate your child's experience of you as unsafe.

Reflections
- *Are there aspects of your child's appearance that they are especially sensitive about?*
- *Are there experiences that your child has had that they would not want you to reference in a message because they would be too embarrassing or painful for them?*
- *Can you remember being the age of your child and feeling worried about what other people think of you, especially your peers?*

KNOW YOUR CHILD
Each child has their own likes and dislikes, preferences, joys, talents, hobbies, and so forth. Try to think about your child as an individual and tailor the message to them as much as possible. For example, if you want to show your love to your child, think about what forms of love are most meaningful to them. Some

people feel most loved through verbal expressions of love such as "I love you to the moon and back." Others are particularly attuned to touch and might be most moved by a message such as "I am sending you warm hugs of love." Yet others appreciate acts of service, in which case, a message of an offer to do something might be particularly appealing such as "How about if I stop by and take your car for a tune-up?" Another form of love is affirmations in which you would describe something positive about them such as "I just saw your report card. Your diligence and hard work really paid off!" Most likely, you want to show your love in a variety of ways throughout your messaging to your child, but always bear in mind your child's preferences.

The encouragement to know your child applies to all aspects of messaging. If your child prefers a certain nickname, then make sure to use that name (or no name at all) rather than insist on using a nickname the child rejects. Don't offer to give or buy your child something they have already told you they don't like (e.g., going out for pizza when they are vegan or buying them a certain brand when they clearly prefer another).

A specific and timely aspect of knowing your child refers to gender pronouns and first names. In today's world, individuals are claiming their own gender identities, sexual orientations, and first names. If your child has told you or you have been informed that your child now considers themselves to be a different name, gender, or orientation than a previous one, it is advised that you use that (or none). Most people do not include first names in text messages because they are not formal letters and there is no need for a salutation such as "Dear Sally." However, if you feel inclined to increase the intensity of a text message by including the child's name (i.e., "Sally, I hope you see . . ."), then we advise that you use the name the child wants to be called. It can be very unsettling to refer to your child by a name that is new and different (especially if you are generally not on board with what the name change represents, e.g., that your child is gay or transgender), but to actively reject your child's self-claimed identity is going to cause them to feel unloved, unknown, and/or unaccepted by you. If you cannot get on board with referring to your child by a new and different name, then we suggest that you avoid using first names at all, especially since it is not necessary for a text message to start with the recipient's name.

Reflections

- *What are some core aspects of your child's identity that do not change regardless of their name, gender identity, and sexual orientation?*
- *What can you do now to know your child better?*
- *How does it feel to know that your child is changing and you are not a part of that process right now?*

DON'T BLAME THE RIFT ON A THIRD PARTY

You probably have strong feelings and clear ideas about what is driving your child to feel hurt, angry, rejecting, and distant. You may believe that the child's other parent is turning your child against you using a range of manipulating strategies and gaslighting (i.e., parental alienation). You might believe that your child's significant other or someone else is controlling them and preventing them from having a relationship with you (because that other individual is narcissistic or sociopathic or has a borderline personality). You may believe that their coach or therapist is manipulating them to believe things about you that are not true. In some instances, there really is a third party who is behind the scenes manipulating and controlling your child. Even in those instances, however, your child most likely sees the situation very differently than you do. Most people who are being manipulated do not see themselves as puppets or objects of manipulation. In fact, most people do not even think that advertising or other obvious forms of influence work on them. If you mention in a message your theory that a third party is manipulating them—usually an individual whom your child loves and is attached to such as a spouse or the other parent—you will be insulting your child and antagonizing them. Any message such as "Can't you see what your [other parent] is doing to you?" or "Why are you letting your [spouse] control you?" will most likely backfire and cause your child to be even more hurt and angry with you. Basically, when you accuse a third party of interfering in the relationship, you are insinuating that your child is a fool or a puppet and cannot think for themselves. You are also insinuating that the third party (i.e., someone whom your child is attached to) is evil and manipulative and probably doesn't really love them. If you send such a message, you are likely to receive a response such as "That is exactly why I don't want you in my life." It is, therefore, recommended that you refrain from referring to your theory of the influence of a third party on your relationship with your child. This includes not sending links to articles, books, podcasts, and such about parental alienation, cults, undue influence, narcissism, borderline personality disorder, sociopathic personality, gaslighting, and all related topics. There may be a time and place to discuss your theory of what happened to the relationship, but a text message to a child who is already hurt, angry, rejecting, and distant is not the right venue for such a conversation.

Reflections

- *How can you help yourself to tolerate the lack of a shared understanding of what happened to cause the rift in the relationship?*

- *How do you experience frustration in your mind and body?*

- *How can you accept and honor those feelings without acting on them in a message to your child?*

Thirty Types of Text Messages

TWENTY-FIVE WAYS TO MESSAGE "I LOVE YOU"

Purpose

IF YOUR RELATIONSHIP WITH YOUR CHILD IS CONFLICTED, MOST likely your child is feeling hurt and angry with you, and the hurt and anger are based on the belief that you are unsafe, unloving, and unavailable even though there may not be much if any truth to this belief. Regardless of the reality of the situation, it is generally helpful to share that feeling of love with your child. It bears repeating—over and over—that your heart is filled with love. You don't want to repeat it day after day because it can seem lazy or hollow, but don't forget to sprinkle these different "I love you" messages throughout your texting repertoire.

Examples

1. I Love You.

2. I luv u.

3. I [image of heart] you so much.

4. You are my precious child and I love you so much.

5. My heart is filled with love for you.

6. I love you yesterday, today, and tomorrow.

7. I love you from the tip of your nose to the tip of your toes.

8. I love you every day whether or not we are together.

9. My love for you has no end.

10. Every day I carry you in my heart.

11. Image of emoji or image of face with hearts for eyes

12. Image of emoji blowing a kiss

13. Image of eye, heart, and ewe

14. I love you to the [image of moon] and back.

15. I loaf [image of loaf of bread] you.

16. Memoji of you as a giraffe blowing kisses to your child

17. Memoji of you as a bunny rabbit winking and saying "I love you"

18. Memoji of you as yourself making a heart sign with your hands

19. A photograph imported from Google Images of a heart drawn into sand on a beach

20. Image of animal parent snuggling with child

21. Image of recognizable cartoon character blowing a kiss

22. Video of a celebrity your child likes saying "I love you"

23. Photo of you blowing your child a kiss

24. Video of you saying "I love you"

25. Video of you blowing your child a kiss

Considerations
- It is important that you don't overly rely on this message because it can seem too easy and therefore, not authentic.
- The message should not be romantic or sexual in any way. Avoid photos of two adults holding hands or kissing.
- The message should not be sad or forlorn in any way. You should not say "I love you so much that I cannot be happy without you" or "I am missing you so much" and include an emoji of a frowning face.
- If you send a photo or video of yourself, make sure to watch it first and screen it for anything that could come across as desperate, sad, grasping, or angry.

Reflections
- *How does your child feel love? Are there certain ways that are more meaningful and special than others?*
- *Are there specific ways that you and your child expressed love to each other?*
- *How does it feel to remember those moments now?*
- *Is there a way to reference them in a message that is appropriate for who your child is today?*
- *How can you feel in your heart that your child still loves you even though they are not willing or able to express that now?*

Fifteen Ways to Message "I Am Thinking about You"
Purpose
Sometimes children who are hurt, angry, rejecting, and distant worry that the distanced parent will move on without them and forget about them. This may seem ironic since it is the child who is actively resisting the relationship, but deep down most children who are hurt, angry, rejecting, and distant want to feel that that parent still loves them no matter what. Your mission is to communicate

your love and commitment to your child so that they don't feel more hurt, anger, rejection, and distance from you, thinking that you have moved on without them. This is why it is a good idea to include an ample dose of "thinking of you" texts in your rotation.

Examples

1. You are on my mind.

2. I am thinking about you today.

3. I am holding you in my heart.

4. You are on my mind, and I am wondering how you are.

5. You are in my [image of heart].

6. [image of emoji thinking] of you!

7. I'm thinking of U.

8. Image of eye, lightbulb, and ewe

9. Image of celebrity (whom your child likes) waving

10. Funny image (such as a cat riding a bicycle saying "I'm thinking about you")

11. Video of you waving to your child

12. Memoji of you as a bunny rabbit waving to your child

13. Memoji of you winking

14. Memoji of you giving the peace sign

15. Photo of you making a peace sign

Considerations

- It is important that the text does not contain any guilt-inducing or seemingly manipulative messaging that would involve implications that you are miserable without the child, such as a video of you looking lost or forlorn, sitting by a rainy window, or eating alone at a restaurant.

- The message also should not convey that you are having too much fun without them, such as a video of you at Disneyland waving to your child. Such a message might convey that you really are having a grand old time without them and don't really miss them at all.

Reflections
- *Are there times of the day when you are more likely to think about your child? Are those good times to send a message, or can you hold the thought for a time that works better for you or for them?*
- *How can you enjoy and savor those memories without being engulfed with grief?*
- *Can you make a list of things that remind you of your child so you can refer to them in your messages as appropriate?*

Ten Ways to Message "I Saw This and Thought of You"
Purpose
This is a more specific version of "thinking of you" in which you see a place or object that contains an association with your child, take a picture or video of it, and send it to your child to let them know that you remember that they like that kind of thing. The purpose of this message is to let your child know that as you go through your day, they are always on your mind. You want to convey to your child that as you walk down the street and move through the world, you are always thinking about them, and because of that, so many things remind you of them.

Examples
Here are some things you might take a photo of and send to your child.

1. A puppy (or other animal your child likes)

2. Display of pastry in bakery window (or other fancy food your child likes)

3. A beautiful flower (or other plant)

4. A lake (or other body of water)

5. Street art (or other work of art your child likes)

6. A stunning or interesting vista

7. A parade (or other interesting gathering of people)

8. A march (or other political event)

9. A coat in a window (or other article of clothing)

10. A rainbow

Considerations
- Make sure not to send a photo of any object you know your child desires (e.g., a necklace or a new Lego set) because it might come across as taunting the child because you know your child would love it but you are not actually buying it for them.

- Don't send a photo of your puppy unless you are sure that it will not come across as manipulative (i.e., your puppy looks sad as if they are missing the child).

- Don't send a photo of something too personal or embarrassing (e.g., their messy bedroom or a wound of yours that is healing).

Reflections
- *Are there certain places, things, and activities that especially remind you of your child?*
- *Can you make a list so that you can refer to them in future messages?*
- *How would it feel if you were to take pictures of these things as you encounter them so that you can share them with your child?*

Ten Ways to Message "Thought You Might Be Interested . . ."

Purpose

This message is a more detailed version of "saw this and thought of you" in that it also shows that you are thinking of your child. The premise of this type of message is that you see something that reminds you of your child and then you share it with them through a message.

Examples
1. A link to a news story about a current event
2. A link to a news story about a celebrity they like
3. A link to a music video
4. A link to a podcast (not one about parental alienation!)
5. A link to a movie review or trailer
6. A link to a promo for a new video game
7. A link to a product review of an item of interest to them
8. A picture of a marquee of a show or movie
9. A picture of a new restaurant
10. A picture of an interesting building

Considerations

- Make sure that the link is a working link.

- Make sure that the link is to an item that would truly be of interest to them—as opposed to of interest to you.

- Make sure that the link is not to a story or item that helps you win an argument. For example, if you believe that XX car is better than YY car, don't send a link to an article about that very subject. It will seem like you are trying to prove a point or win an argument—as opposed to trying to connect.

- Make sure that the link is not to an item that is violent or sexist or not age appropriate.

- Remember to avoid links to articles, videos, books, and podcasts that reference your theory about how a third party is interfering in your relationship with them.

Reflections

- *What are some topics that are especially interesting and important to your child?*

- *What are some things that you did together or talked about that you can reference in a message?*

- *What are some common interests that you shared and appreciated together in a meaningful way?*

- *Are there topics that you might want to avoid?*

TEN WAYS TO MESSAGE A GENERAL INVITATION

Purpose

The purpose of the general invitation is to show your child that you would like to have contact but that you are not trying to pin them down to a specific commitment. You are suggesting things that the child generally likes to do to show them that you are thinking of them (see above) and know them enough to know what they like. The invitation also conveys that you are not giving up on reconnecting with your child and that you will always be hoping to spark an interest in them to be together again.

Examples

1. Want to see the new [insert] movie sometime?

2. Any interest in going for a hike [or doing some other activity]?

3. Wanna get some [image of specific food such as sushi or some other cuisine]?

4. Wanna get some [image of dessert such as ice cream cone] with me?

5. [image of movie ticket] + [image of popcorn] with me?

6. Want to take a walk sometime?

7. [image of ice skating or some other sport]?

8. I would love to get together and hang out and talk or whatever you want.

9. What do you think about my visiting you sometime?

10. Can we get together sometime this [season]?

Considerations

- Make sure not to suggest things that you cannot deliver on. For example, don't invite your child skiing unless you plan to take them skiing.

- Make sure not to suggest things that your child does not like (e.g., offering sushi when your child does not care for sushi).

Reflections

- *What are some of your child's activities and interests that you can invite them to?*

- *How can you remind yourself that the invitation is just one grain of sand and that you don't expect to hear back?*

- *Can you visualize the invitation like a message in a bottle tossed into the ocean, not knowing how it will make its way to your child's heart?*

- *Can you remind yourself that it is the offer that matters, not the response, because the offer is a way to show your child that you love them regardless of whether they are able or willing in that moment to acknowledge and reciprocate?*

TEN WAYS TO MESSAGE A SPECIFIC INVITATION

Purpose

Like the general invitation, the purpose of the specific invitation is to show your child that you want to have contact. However, in this instance you are offering something specific to see if you can get a commitment from them to spend time with you. You are suggesting things that the child is highly likely to want to do to show them that you are thinking of them (see above) and know them enough to know what they like.

Examples

1. I am on my way to Starbucks [or other coffee place]. Can I pick you up a latte? [image of cup of coffee]

2. Want to see the new Star Wars movie this weekend? [image of popcorn]

3. I am planning on picking up tacos for dinner. Want to join me? [image of taco] + [image of a thumbs up]

4. Want to come by and visit the [image of your pet]?

5. Want to come over for [image of eggs in a pan] or [image of stack of pancakes] tomorrow morning?

6. I'm getting tickets to the [name of sports team] game on Friday. Want to join me?

7. I'm free this morning. Want to take a walk?

8. Want to [image of shooting hoops] today?

9. Want to do some baking together on Sunday?

10. How about dinner tonight?

Considerations

- Make sure not to suggest things that you cannot deliver on. For example, don't invite your child out for dinner that night if you don't have the time or money to go out to dinner.

- Make sure not to suggest things that your child does not like (e.g., offering a particular brand of drink or food when your child prefers something else).

- Make sure that you are prepared to do the activity even if your child is sullen or quiet or just doesn't want to talk about the relationship.

Reflections

- *Would it help to prepare yourself for a lack of response so that you are not despondent if no response comes?*

- *How would it feel to do the activity without your child? Would you still be able to enjoy the game, movie, concert, or whatever?*

- *Would it be helpful to visualize a time in the future when you are once again spending time with your child?*

FIFTEEN WAYS TO MESSAGE "HAVE A GREAT DAY"

Purpose

Even though your child is angry with and rejecting you, that does not mean that you wish your child ill. However, your child may imagine that you are angry with them, and therefore, it is helpful to remind your child through your messages that you are hoping that they are okay and in a good frame of mind. This message can be sent to show your child that you are thinking of them and hoping that their life is going well and that they are happy and having a good time. It shows your child that—even though they are rejecting you—you don't wish them any ill. In fact, quite the opposite. Because you love them you want them to be happy no matter what.

Examples

1. Good morning! I hope you have a wonderful day.

2. Hiya [appropriate nickname]. Hope U have a great day. [image of a thumbs up]

3. Here's hoping the day is a good one for you.

4. I hope the day brings you everything you want it to.

5. May this day bring you joy and happiness.

6. I hope this day brings you love and happiness.

7. I hope you have an amazing day today!

8. Hopin' ur day is great!

9. [image of praying hands] for a good [image of a calendar day]

10. Image of a polar bear waving and saying "Have a great day"

11. Image of kitten hanging upside down saying "Have a good day"

12. Animated image of the words "Enjoy your day"

13. Memoji of you as a polar bear waving and saying "Have a good one"

14. Memoji of you winking and saying "Have a good one"

15. Video of you saying "Have a great day"

Considerations
- Make sure that you don't convey sadness over missing the child. In other words, don't look sad in the photo or video of yourself that you send, and/or don't add "even though we are not together" because that could appear to be guilt inducing.
- If you know something is going on with your child that will make the day very hard for them (e.g., they are in the hospital or are speaking with the custody evaluator), it might seem bizarre to send a "have a great day" message.

Reflections
- *Can you wish yourself a wonderful day as well as your child since you deserve it as much as anyone else?*
- *Can you imagine having a wonderful day even if you don't hear back from your child? What would make it so?*
- *What is a great day for your child? Can you reference something specific that has meaning to them?*

TEN WAYS TO MESSAGE "I HOPE YOU HAD A GOOD DAY"
Purpose
As noted above, your child might imagine that you are angry with them because they are hurt, angry, rejecting, and distant and perhaps you are hoping that their life is going badly. Therefore, it is helpful to remind your child through your messages that you are

hoping that they are okay and in a good frame of mind. This message can be sent at the end of the day as a final thought of the day.

Examples

1. I hope you had a lovely day.

2. I hope your day was great.

3. Hoping your day was a good one.

4. Hope your [image of a calendar day] was excellent!

5. I [image of praying hands] U had a [image of hands making A-OK sign] day.

6. Hoping ur day was [image of thumbs up].

7. I hope your day was A-OK.

8. Video of you saying "I hope you had a wonderful day"

9. Memoji of you as a giraffe saying "Hope you had a great day"

10. Memoji of you saying "Hope your day was excellent!"

Considerations (these are the same as above since this topic is a variation of the one above)

- Make sure that you don't convey sadness over missing the child. In other words, don't look sad in the photo or video of yourself that you send, and/or don't add "even though we have not been together" because that could appear to be guilt inducing.

- If you know something is going on with your child that would have made the day very hard for them (e.g., they are in the hospital or are speaking with the custody evaluator), it might seem bizarre to send a "hope you a great day" message.

Reflections

- *How was your day? Were you able to focus on aspects of your child that are rewarding to you?*

- *What would have made the day better—aside from reconnecting with your child? What can you do to make tomorrow better?*

- *What can you do right now to help you feel better?*

FIFTEEN WAYS TO MESSAGE "GOOD NIGHT"

Purpose

Most parents say good night to their children every day of their life—even during periods of separation (e.g., sleep-away camp, sleepovers, or separation/divorce). Tucking the child in at night can be a very sweet and tender moment between parent and child. It offers the parent an opportunity to send the child into sleep with a feeling of love and connection. However, if there is a partial or total cut off from the child, suddenly the parent does not have that opportunity to share that end-of-the-day moment of connection. Sending a message of good night might be the best or only option available.

Examples

1. Good night, sweetheart.

2. Good night, my precious child.

3. GN [image of heart]

4. Sending love and kisses at bedtime.

5. Sending [image of heart] at the end of the day

6. Sweet dreams.

7. I hope you have sweet dreams.

8. Good [image of sleeping Zs]

9. Good [image of nighttime]

10. [image of thumbs up] + [image of bedtime]

11. Memoji of you waving with the text "Good night, honey"

12. Video of you saying "sweet dreams"

13. Image of a celebrity your child likes saying "Good night"

14. Image of a unicorn in bed snoozing

15. Image of a puppy falling asleep

Considerations

- Make sure that you don't convey sadness over missing the child. In other words, don't look sad in the photo or video of yourself that you send, and/or don't add "even though we are not together" because that could appear to be guilt inducing.

Reflections

- *What special routines did you and your child have at bedtime? Can you reference some of those elements in your message?*

- *Did or does your child have a special stuffed animal that was or is cuddled at bedtime? Can you reference that in your message in a way that is developmentally appropriate?*

- *What can you do for yourself to ensure that you have a lovely night's sleep so that you can be fortified for whatever tomorrow brings?*

TEN WAYS TO MESSAGE AFTER SEEING THE CHILD PARTICIPATE IN AN ACTIVITY

Purpose

Even parents who are cut off from their child sometimes have opportunities to observe their child participate in or perform in activities. If the child is school aged, this could involve a school concert your child is playing in, a school play your child has a part in, an athletic game or event in which your child participates, or an academic competition your child is involved in. It could also involve a religious event (e.g., communion or graduation from Sunday school) or even something in the community (e.g., a volunteer event). If you have an opportunity to observe your child, you probably want to follow up with a positive response to them.

Examples

1. Great game/show/performance today!

2. I love to watch you play/sing/perform/etc. [image of smiling face]

3. What a joy to see you play/sing/perform/etc.

4. You put your heart into everything you do. [image of heart]

5. I am so proud of you.

6. I am so glad I had a chance to catch your game/performance.

7. You really gave it your all. I'm so proud of you.

8. You looked terrific on the field/stage/debate team/etc.

9. Memoji of you as a puppy saying "What a great game/performance/debate/etc."

10. Memoji of you blowing kisses or giving a thumbs up and saying "Fantastic performance/show/debate/etc. today"

Considerations

- Ideally, you should keep the focus on the effort rather than the product or outcome. In other words, whether your child won or lost should not be the focus of your message.

- If there is a restraining order and/or you have agreed not to attend, then you should not indicate that you were there by following up with a message. Of course, you should not violate any restraining orders.

- If your child had a particularly good performance (e.g., scored a goal, saved the game, hit all the high notes, made outstanding points in the debate, or did a great solo), it would make sense to mention it.

- If the child really had a bad day (e.g., lost the game or forgot their lines), you might want to mention something like "Tough game today, but you gave it your all" or "Even though the other team won, it looked to me like you had some good plays in there."

Reflections
- *How can you express pride and pleasure in who your child is rather than in what they have achieved?*
- *How can you convey support for your child even if their performance was disappointing for them?*
- *Can you feel pride in your child's efforts and strivings? Does that help you feel proud of your efforts to strive to reconnect with your child even though you have not yet achieved your goal?*

TEN WAYS TO MESSAGE "CONGRATULATIONS!"
Purpose
You may have opportunities to learn that your child has achieved a milestone or reached an important accomplishment. Regardless of the nature of the relationship, sending a message of congratulations shows that you are proud of and love them and are aware of things going on in their life. As with other messages, this helps to counter the lie that you don't care.

Examples

1. Congratulations on your report card/ranking/honor society. I'm so proud of you! [image of party hat and confetti]

2. Bravo! What a great performance last night! [image of clapping hands]

3. Another great performance by a great player. [image of football or other relevant item]

4. You must be feeling proud of yourself right now. I know I would be. [image of proud emoji]

5. Hats off to you for another great performance. [image of fun hat]

6. Congratulations for your college acceptance/promotion. Well deserved!!

7. I heard you got picked for the team/play/orchestra/etc. What an honor!

8. Congrats to you. What a great student you have been. [image of graduation cap and image of confetti]

9. Image of the word "congratulations" exploding in fireworks

10. A memoji of a puppy saying "Congratulations!!!"

Considerations

- Make sure that the focus is on the process as much as the outcome.
- Make sure that it is okay for you to know about the accomplishment. Otherwise, it could seem as if you are stalking them, and that could come off as creepy or intrusive.

Reflections

- *What are some ways that you congratulated the child in the past?*

- *How does it feel to know your child has achieved something and you have not had an opportunity to share in the experience in a truly connected and meaningful way?*

- *Would it help to write some memories of today in a journal so you can share it with your child later, including small but meaningful details about their success/accomplishment?*

TEN WAYS TO MESSAGE "GOOD LUCK"

Purpose

It is important for your child to know that you are rooting for them even though they are hurt, angry, rejecting, and distant in their relationship with you. If you know there is something going on in your child's life that feels high stakes (i.e., it is important for your child to accomplish something), then it is appropriate for you to say that you are thinking of them and hoping that they get the outcome they are hoping for. You are showing that their hopes and dreams are also your hopes and dreams; you are in their corner rooting for them. Here are some examples of things you might want to check in about: a math test, finals at school, the SATs, a doctor's visit, first day of camp, field trip, job interview, college application, getting braces on or off, getting a cast on or off, getting a new phone, getting a car, taking the driver's test, going to prom, or graduating.

Examples

1. Good luck on your [event] today. [image of fingers crossed]

2. Thinking of you on your big day today. [image of fingers crossed]

3. Here's hoping the [event] goes well. [image of smiling emoji]

4. Hope all goes well with your [event] today. [image of four-leaf clover]

5. I know you have your [event] coming up. I hope it all goes the way you want it to. [image of emoji with heart eyes]

6. I'm thinking of you today. I hope it all goes well. [image of heart]

7. Image of cartoon character saying "I'm rooting for you"

8. Image of the words "Good Luck" spelled out on the sand of a beach

9. Memoji of you giving a thumbs-up sign saying "Good luck"

10. Memoji of you as a giraffe saying "Good luck"

Considerations

- You don't want to seem overly enthusiastic about something that doesn't mean that much to your child because that could come across as micromanaging or trying too hard.

- If you have been accused of being too focused on grades and school performance, it would not be advisable for you to send a message wishing them good luck on a test because that would reinforce that idea.

Reflections

- *Do you feel that you have been particularly unlucky in your life to end up with a hurt, angry, rejecting, distant child? Can you keep your feelings of bitterness and frustration out of your message?*

- *Do you feel that a message of well-wishing would show that your child is doing well without you—something that may be painful or inconvenient to acknowledge?*

- *How can you set those feelings aside so you can demonstrate to your child that you celebrate their successes because you love them?*

TEN WAYS TO ASK "HOW DID IT GO?"

Purpose

If you message your child wishing them good luck on an upcoming important event, then it would only make sense that you would follow up to ask how it went and to express your interest and support. If you don't, it could seem as if you don't really care. Here are some examples of things you might want to check in about: a math test, finals at school, the SATs, a doctor's visit, first day of camp, field trip, job interview, college application, getting braces on or off, getting a cast on or off, getting a new phone, getting a car, taking the driver's test, going to prom, or graduating.

Examples

1. How did the [event] go? [image of curious emoji]

2. Hey, just checking in to say I hope the [event] went well. [image of fingers crossed]

3. How did you feel the [event] went for you?

4. Are you pleased with how things turned out with the [event]?

5. I am curious how it all worked out with the [event]. [image of curious cat]

6. I was thinking about you while the [event] was going on. How'd it go?

7. I hope the [event] went well yesterday.

8. So??? Any news? [image of newspaper]

9. Image of cute animal saying "How'd it go?"

10. Memoji of you looking curious saying "Just checking in . . ."

Considerations (these are the same as above since the topic is similar to the one above)

- You don't want to seem overly enthusiastic about something that doesn't mean that much to your child because that can come across as micromanaging or trying too hard.

- If you have been accused of being too focused on grades and school performance, it would not be advisable for you to send a message asking them how it went with the test because that would just reinforce that idea.

Reflections

- *How will your child feel if you follow up about something they were involved with? Will it feel like you are too invested in their achievements?*

- *How can you convey your interest in your child's day-to-day life without seeming to micromanage or be overly focused on outcomes?*

- *How do you feel about your child's achievements while they are hurt, angry, rejecting, and distant from you?*

TEN WAYS TO MESSAGE A SICK CHILD
Purpose
If your child has been ill, it is important that you follow up to see how they are feeling. It shows that you are thinking of them, you care about them, and you are nurturing them and have love in your heart for them.

Examples

1. How's your tummy/throat/etc. feeling today? [image of loving emoji]

2. I hope you're feeling better. [image of smiling emoji]

3. I am sending healing thoughts your way. [image of emoji blowing kiss]

4. Sending thoughts of chicken soup (or some other food that signifies caretaking) your way! Hope you feel better soon. [image of bowl of soup]

5. Hope your fever is down. [image of emoji taking temperature]

6. Image of favorite celebrity saying "Feel better soon"

7. Memoji of you sending healing thoughts

8. Image of the words "Here's hoping you are on the mend!"

9. Image of a bunny hopping with the words "Here's hopping you are feeling better"

10. Message saying that you sent a care package to their address (if they do not live with the favored parent). The care package could be some combination of the following items: soup, essential oils, fuzzy slippers, puzzle magazines, chocolate covered strawberries, or whatever you think would feel warm and nurturing to your child.

Considerations

• Of course, you want to tailor the message to the seriousness of the illness. If your child is very ill, it would seem callous and possibly bizarre to send a message of a bunny saying "Here's hopping you are feeling better" or some other playful message.

- If the child is very ill, it could also be advised that you reach out to the other parent, or the child's spouse/roommate if they are an adult and live with someone else, to receive a status update and to see if you can be involved in medical decisions and/or possibly visit the child. Under those circumstances, a message alone (without the phone call and offer to visit) would also likely seem as if you don't really care.

Reflections
- *When they were young, how did your child like to be cared for when they were sick (e.g., lots of snuggles or lots of time to be alone and sleep)?*
- *Were there any specific gestures (e.g., feeling their forehead with your lips) that you did as part of your caretaking routine?*
- *Is there a way to send a care package, and if so, what would you put in it to show that you know your child and understand who they are and what would feel nurturing and cheer them up?*

Ten Ways to Message an Offer to Buy Something
Purpose
Whether you have an ongoing relationship or not, your child is still growing and changing and developing new interests and talents. Your child is likely to need something or is interested in obtaining something; if you are in a position to purchase that for your child, here are some ways to go about doing that.

Examples
1. Hey, just checking in. Do you want a new laptop before you begin the new school year/high school/college? I would be happy to buy one for you.

2. How are you set for a winter jacket? I would love to pick one up for you before it gets too cold. [image of snowflake]

3. Want to go to [name of store] and get some school supplies before the school year starts? [image of paperclip, folders, etc.]

4. I am heading to [store]. Anything you want me to pick up for you?

5. I saw a really cute [item]. Would you like one?

6. If I were to get you a new pair of sneakers, what style, brand, and size would you want? [image of sneakers]

7. If you are still into [hobby], I can pick up a new [item] for you this weekend. What do you say?? [image of thumbs up]

8. I am heading to the bookstore. Are you interested in reading the latest in the [name] series? Can I get that for you?

9. I hear that [fad] is in right now. Can I get you one?

10. I hear that [event] is coming up. What do you need that I can get for you?

Considerations

- Make sure not to offer to buy something that you cannot afford or do not want to purchase for your child.

- Make sure that you are all in or else put some limits on the offer. For example, some pairs of sneakers can be very pricey as are some prom dresses and laptops.

- Make sure that the item is not so big that before buying, you should really check with the other parent or your child's spouse/roommate if your child is an adult and lives with someone else (e.g., a new car for the child) because the item could create conflict and/or expense for them (e.g., car insurance or a space in the garage or driveway).

- Don't offer to buy something that interferes with the other parent's discretion or authority such as Wi-Fi or a TV for the child's home (if the child still lives with the other parent) because that other parent has a right to say that they don't want you buying their Wi-Fi or they don't want the child to have a TV in their room.

Reflections
- *What is something your child needs that you might be able to buy for them?*
- *How would it feel for you to spend the time and money on the object for them when you might not receive the kind of gratitude that you would like or think is due in the situation?*
- *Can you make the offer to purchase the item for them with a pure heart, not looking for anything in return?*

TEN WAYS TO MESSAGE AN OFFER TO GIVE SOMETHING
Purpose
If you are like other parents with hurt, angry, rejecting, distant children, you probably have objects that you have accumulated over time that you think would be of interest to your child. It may be something you own and are ready to pass down to them (e.g., a car, a specialized tool, or a piece of artwork). It might be that your child has left something in the home that you think they might want or you have received something for the child from someone else who is not in touch with the child (e.g., a friend or relative of yours).

Examples
1. I found your old [object]. Would you like to have it?

2. [Name of person] has a gift for you. How can I get it to you?

3. I am ready to pass on my [object]. Interested?

4. I came across an [object]. Would you like to have it?

5. Someone passed a(n) [object] on to me, and I thought you might want it.

6. What would you say to having my [object]?

7. Just a reminder that your [object] is still here and you can have it whenever you want it.

8. I have collected some [objects] over the years and wanted to know if you wanted them.

9. If you ever want to come and pick up your [object], just let me know. It is here for you.

10. [Name] gave me a(n) [object] for you. Can I drop by and give it to you?

Considerations

- Make sure not to offer your child something that you cannot afford to give them (most likely, passing down a car requires that you get yourself a new one) or is something that you do not want to give to them.

- Make sure that you are all in or else put some limits on the offer. For example, if you intend to loan your child the object, make sure that you are very clear about that up front. Any misunderstanding could reflect poorly on you and reinforce your child feeling hurt and angry with you.

- Make sure that the object is in good shape or if not, that you are clear about that. For example you could say "Hey, I found your old violin in the closet. It may need some sprucing up, but you can come get it whenever you want to."

- Make sure that the item is not so big that you should check with the other parent first (e.g., buying a new car

for the child) because the item could create conflict and/
or expense for them (e.g., car insurance or a space in the
garage or driveway).

- Don't offer something that interferes with the other
  parent's discretion such as offering to buy Wi-Fi or a TV
  for the child's home (if the child still lives with the other
  parent) because that other parent has a right to say that
  they don't want you buying their Wi-Fi or they don't want
  the child to have a TV in their room.

Reflections

- *What do you have that you can give or share with your child that might show them that you are thinking of them?*
- *How would it feel for you to not have the object in your possession anymore? Can you take a photo or make a copy so that you have a way to look at it yourself?*
- *Can you make the offer with a pure heart, not looking for anything in return?*

TEN WAYS TO MESSAGE AN OFFER TO FIX SOMETHING

Purpose

As time goes by, things your child owns might break or wear
down and need repair. Even though your child is rejecting you,
nothing is stopping you from asking them if they need some
assistance in repairing something. Such a message shows that you
are thinking about your child, you care about them, and you are
willing to invest time and energy (and perhaps money) to assist
with a repair.

Examples

1. How's the car running? Everything okay? [image of car]

2. Want me to come around sometime and show you how to change the oil/tires/etc.?

3. If you ever want a suggestion for a mechanic, let me know.

4. How's your dolly/favorite stuffed animal/etc.? [image of doll]

5. How's your computer holding up? [image of computer]

6. How's the new phone working? Any glitches I can assist with? [image of phone]

7. Any repairs I can help out with around the home/apartment? (assuming the child does not live with the other parent)

8. How's the bike holding up? Everything still working okay? [image of bike]

9. I would be happy to come around sometime and do some minor repairs if you want. (assuming they do not live with the other parent)

10. How's that leaky faucet? Need a hand with that?

Considerations

- Make sure that you are not offering to fix something that you cannot fix. You certainly don't want to offer to fix something and then have to back out because it exceeds your skill set. You also do not want to offer to fix something and then actually make the problem worse (unless you are fully prepared to repair whatever problem you create with your efforts).

- Make sure that you are not offering to fix something you don't have the time to fix because reneging on that could create the impression that you are untrustworthy.

Reflections
- *How would it feel for you to do the repair and not be thanked and appreciated the way you think the situation warrants?*
- *What is your hope for how the situation will go if your child does take you up on the offer? What can you do to bring that vision closer to reality?*

TEN WAYS TO MESSAGE NEWS THAT IS EASY TO SHARE
Purpose

The world is still going on around you and your child even while you are cut off from each other. One way to connect is to comment on something happening that is relevant to the child. It could be a local event, something big in politics, or something that is going on with someone you both know.

Examples

1. I just heard Aunt Sally is having a baby. How exciting! [image of baby]

2. I just heard you got a new puppy. Woof! [image of puppy]

3. I just heard they are closing the roller rink. Bummer! [image of crying face]

4. I just heard [name of favorite drink] is back at [name of coffee shop]. [image of happy face]

5. I just heard a [name of store] is coming to [name of town]. [image of thumbs up]

6. I just heard there is a new [name of movie franchise]. [image of popcorn]

7. I just heard [favorite celebrity] is getting married. What do you think?

8. I just heard they closed [name of street]. Everything okay?

9. I just heard your dance studio got voted best in the county. How exciting!

10. I just heard [pop star] is dropping a new single today. What do you think?

Considerations

- For the most part, the news should be positive or only mildly negative. If it were very negative or highly charged for the child, that would require a different kind of text (see below).

- For the most part, the news should not be about the child achieving something because that would require a different kind of response (i.e., congratulations or condolences).

- Don't send a message about something happening in the world that you and your child are in conflict over. For example, if there is a political march on a topic you don't agree on, don't bring it up.

Reflections

- *How does sharing news by message rather than in person feel? What does it mean to you?*

- *How are you coping with the reality that the world moves on even though you are stuck in the terrible situation of being cut off from or in conflict with your beloved child?*

- *Is there some way to memorialize the news (e.g., photos of the new puppies) to share with your child when the time is right?*

Ten Ways to Message News That Is Hard to Share
Purpose
You might find yourself in a position to have news about a friend or relative on your side of the family, news that your child would not otherwise know about because they are not in touch with your

friends and relatives. If you think it is important to have your child know about the news, you can send them a message about it. The rule of thumb is to send a message if you believe that your child would be hurt and angry if you failed to let them know about the news and/or your friend/relative would be hurt/angry if you did not pass on the news. The news itself may be bad (e.g., illness or death), or it could be hard to share because the child will have feelings hearing about it. For example, if the child is cut off from a sibling, even positive news about that sibling could be painful to hear. Likewise, if the child's dog at your house has puppies— something that is generally happy news—it still may be hard for the child to hear the news since they were not there for the big event.

Examples

1. [Name] had her baby yesterday! There were some problems; call me if you want to hear the details.

2. Thought you would want to know that [name] had some medical tests last week and it looks like there are some problems. Please call them or me for details.

3. News flash: Sunshine had her puppies today. So cute! Mommy and puppies are all healthy. Let me know if you want to see some pics.

4. Update: [name] is feeling much better and will be discharged tomorrow. [image of clapping hands]

5. Did you hear that [name] slipped and broke [bone]? They are at [name] hospital in case you can visit.

6. [Name] got engaged yesterday! [image of ring] I thought you would want to know.

7. [Name] is leaving for [place] next week. Thought you might want to know.

8. I have some sad news about [name]. Please call me so I can share with you on the phone.

9. [Name] is not doing too well, and I thought you might want to drop by in the next day or two if you can.

10. I have some important news to share, and I wanted to speak to you. Can we please talk on the phone today or tomorrow?

Considerations
- You want to make sure that you are not manipulating the child. Only ask to speak to them in person if it is big news (e.g., you are moving, getting married, or having a baby) or bad news (e.g., someone is very sick or has passed away).
- Be very mindful of how your child will receive the news, and make sure to reassure them, for example, by letting them know that the dog is okay after giving birth.

Reflections
- *Do you have some private wish that perhaps sharing the news will bring you and your child closer?*
- *How will you manage and process your anger if your child does not respond to the news in the way that you had hoped (e.g., visiting the relative in the hospital or attending the funeral)?*
- *Is there a way for you to capture the moment (e.g., photos, videos, or journaling) so that you can share it with your child when the time is right?*

TEN WAYS TO SEND A BABY PHOTO
Purpose
Children usually like to see pictures of themselves when they were younger, so every once in a while, you can send a copy of a photo like that along with a message about how cute, delightful,

and adorable they were. Below are some ideas about messages that could accompany such a picture.

Examples

1. You were such a cutie pie!

2. What a sweet baby you were! [image of heart]

3. Look at those eyes, so bright and curious!

4. I came across this photo and wanted to share it with you.

5. You were so adorable. [image of smiling face]

6. Here you are in the ocean for the first time. You loved the water! [image of fish]

7. Your first birthday cake. Yummy! [image of cake]

8. What a sweet big sister/brother you were!

9. Your first time on a bike! [image of bike]

10. Here's a picture of you with [pet]—so sweet!

Considerations

- Avoid photos that include you, especially those that show your child being positive/affectionate with you because it could appear that you are trying to prove that your child once loved you and therefore couldn't possibly have a legitimate reason to be mad at you now.

- Avoid photos that your child would find embarrassing such as being naked, in the bathtub, or picking their nose. Teens especially can be highly sensitive to looking "bad," and you wouldn't want to induce feelings of shame or embarrassment in them.

Reflections
- *What thoughts and feelings are brought up when you look at baby photos? Are you reminded of your hopes and dreams (and assumptions) of what your relationship would be like?*

- *Does it help to remind yourself that you don't have to look at the photos if they bring you too much pain?*

- *Does it help to remind yourself that every situation is unique and there are no rules as to whether you should or should not look at baby photos of your hurt, angry, rejecting, distant child?*

TEN WAYS TO MESSAGE ABOUT A SHARED MEMORY
Purpose
Parents are filled with shared memories of times they spent with their child. When there is a cut off or extreme conflict and distance in a relationship, it can sometimes help to remember prior positive times together. Every so often, you can send a message about a shared memory to show your child that you remember those times.

Examples
1. Remember this movie? [logo of movie] You had so much fun seeing it on the big screen!

2. I went to [name of restaurant] and thought about that time you tried [food].

3. Saw this cupcake and thought about that time you made cupcakes for the whole class.

4. I was walking at [name of park] and thought about that time we saw the swans.

5. I saw this [item of clothing] and remembered your old [beloved item of clothing].

6. I watched [name of movie], and it reminded me of how much you loved going to [name of place].

7. Remember the time we tried to make [name of food] from scratch? [image of surprised face]

8. Remember when we went to that [name of store] and you found that beautiful [item]?

9. I saw this [item of clothing] and remembered how much you loved to wear your [item of clothing].

10. Remember when we flew that kite in [name of park]?

Considerations

- You want to make sure that the memory is a good memory for your child, so you wouldn't want to reminisce about a time that was embarrassing or painful for them.

- You want to make sure that the memory is not designed to cast you in an idealized light such as "Remember the time I took all your friends to the movies?" or "Remember the time I helped you bake one hundred cupcakes?" The purpose is not to remind the child that you are fantastic, only that you have a shared history that is meaningful to you—and hopefully, to them as well.

Reflections

- *Can you share a memory and hold at bay the wish that it will spark an immediate desire or reaction from the child?*

- *We invite you to remind yourself that your child may have a different memory of the event or situation than you do.*

- *Would it help to keep a memory journal to jot down some memories when they come to you so that you can draw on them in future texts?*

Ten Ways to Message a Joke, a Riddle, or a Game
Purpose
Sometimes it helps to insert a little levity into a conflicted relationship, so from time to time, telling a joke or riddle is a fine way to communicate with a hurt, angry, rejecting, distant child. Also, if you only tell the first part, then your child might be intrigued enough to play along.

Examples
1. Get a riddle book and copy in the first part such as "What did the XX say to the XX?" or "Did you hear the one about the guy who . . .?"

2. "Knock knock."

3. Go to a website of visual brain teasers and copy and paste one into your message.

4. Send a link to a game (e.g., Wordle or Semantle).

5. Invite your child to play a mutual game on your phone (e.g., Words with Friends).

6. Provide your child with the clues of a "lateral puzzle" and wait to see if they ask you any yes/no questions to solve the mystery.

7. Start a game of twenty questions by texting "I'm thinking of something. Can you guess what it is in under twenty questions? All questions must be yes/no."

8. Play virtual I spy by texting "I am thinking of your bedroom here, and I see something red. Can you guess what it is?"

9. Send a baby picture of someone and ask "Who is this a baby picture of?"

10. Go to a website with word brain teasers and copy and paste one into your message.

Considerations

- Make sure your jokes and puzzles are age appropriate because a joke that seems funny to a seven-year-old would be insulting for a teenager or adult, and likewise, a brain teaser that is engaging for a young adult would be frustrating and confusing for a younger child.

- Make sure that the riddles, jokes, and games are not violent, sexist, or insulting to your child's sensibilities (e.g., if your child is a vegan, don't invite them to play a game that involves eating animals).

Reflections

- *How would it feel for you to inject playfulness and humor into your messages?*

- *Are there certain types of humor that your child enjoys more than others?*

- *Can you find joy and humor in your day even though your child is hurt, angry, rejecting, and distant?*

TEN WAYS TO MESSAGE ABOUT A RECIPE

Purpose

Providing and sharing food is one way that parents nurture and care for their children. Most cutoff parents cannot literally provide or share meals with their children, but they can do the next best thing, which is to reference food in their texts. The smells and tastes of food can also trigger positive memories, so references to foods your child likes can not only place you in the role of a virtual nurturer, but it can also create a positive association between that food and you.

Examples

1. Just a thought. . . . Have you ever tried adding [novel ingredient] to your famous chocolate chip cookies? [image of a cookie]

2. I'm trying to recreate [restaurant's dish] with [novel ingredient]. How do you think that will go?

3. I would love to make your [dish]. Do you have a recipe I could have?

4. I came across this recipe and thought you might like to try it out.

5. How about this for an interesting recipe?

6. I just learned the right way to smash garlic. Who knew? [image of chagrined face]

7. I just made [dish], and it came out so yummy! Here's the recipe in case you want to try it out. Let me know how it goes.

8. I know you love to make [dish], so I am passing this recipe along in case you want to add it to your collection.

9. Hey, I was just thinking about [dish]. Have you made that recently? I bet it's as good as ever. [image of face licking its lips]

10. Did you know that you can substitute [ingredient] for [ingredient] when making [dish]? Have you ever tried that?

Considerations
- Most of these make sense only for a child who is interested in food and/or likes to cook.
- Make sure not to imply that you know how to do something better than your child.

Reflections
- *What role has food and food preparation played in your relationship with your child?*

- *Are there certain tastes and smells that would bring back positive memories for them?*

- *Is feeding and food preparation one way that you expressed nurturance and care for your child when they were growing up? What are some other ways?*

TEN WAYS TO MESSAGE ABOUT THE WEATHER
Purpose
Weather is all around us and something we all experience every day in a very visceral way, so it is an easy topic of conversation. Young kids especially are enchanted and interested in the weather. Weather can also be a reference for our moods and internal states (e.g., cloudy, dreary, sunny, warm, or cold), so it functions as a metaphor of emotional connection.

Examples
1. Looks like a sunny day. [image of sun]

2. I see the sun in the sky, the same sun that is shining on both of us.

3. On this warm day, I am sending warm hugs your way.

4. Uh oh. Looks like rain. [image of umbrella]

5. [image of rain] [image of rainbow]

6. Snow! [image of snowflake] [image of snowman]

7. Image of snowman

8. Brrr, chilly day. I am sending warm hugs your way!

9. Image of celebrity sending hugs

10. Video of you saying "I am sending you warm hugs"

Consideration

- Some weather emojis can seem babyish, and you want to make sure that you don't come across as out of touch with your child as they grow up.

Reflections

- *Are there certain types of weather that your child particularly enjoys?*

- *Does it help to remind yourself that you and your child are sharing the same weather (assuming you live near each other) and that the same sun, moon, wind, and stars that you see and feel are also experienced by your child? Does that create a feeling of closeness?*

FORTY WAYS TO MESSAGE HOLIDAY WISHES

Purpose

Celebrating holidays with children is usually a very joyful experience for parents. Children are so enthusiastic about special events, and sharing special events can help families create rituals and routines (e.g., always making a particular recipe for a particular holiday or decorating the house a certain way). This increases the feeling of belonging among family members. Even if you are separated from your child, it is still important to acknowledge special days—especially if they are important to your child—and it certainly offers an easy excuse to send a message.

Examples

1. Happy New Year! I hope the new year brings you all good things. [image of party hat and confetti]

2. It's New Year's Day. I'm getting my resolutions together. [image of thoughtful expression]

3. An image of fireworks

4. Happy Valentine's Day. My heart is filled with love for you. Sending you love and chocolate. [image of chocolate] [image of hearts] (Of course, if it makes sense to send real chocolate, that would be good too.)

5. Happy [image of heart] day. You are in my heart!

6. An image of a celebrity blowing a kiss

7. It's St. Pat's Day today. I'm sending you love and four-leaf clovers for luck. [image of four-leaf clover]

8. Are you going to wear something green today in honor of St. Patrick's Day?

9. Image of a leprechaun dancing and singing Happy St. Patrick's Day

10. Happy Easter! I'm thinking about bunnies and Easter eggs and you! [image of bunny]

11. It's Easter!! I hope you have a lovely day!

12. An image of a bunny leaping in the air

13. Happy Memorial Day today! The unofficial start of summer [image of sun and face with sunglasses]

14. An image that says "May the Fourth be with you"

15. A memoji of a dolphin splashing in the ocean

16. Yay, it's Flag Day! [image of flag]

17. First day of summer! Yay! [image of sun]

18. Image of someone dancing on the beach

19. Happy Independence Day! [image of fireworks]

20. Hope you have a great day to celebrate freedom and democracy. [image of Statue of Liberty]

21. Have a great Fourth!

22. Happy Monday! I hope it's a great one!

23. Image of a celebrity saying "Yay! It's Monday"

24. Memoji of you saying "Have a great Monday"

25. Happy Labor Day! [image of person working]

26. Have a great last day of summer! [image of sunset]

27. Memoji of you as a polar bear saying "Happy Labor Day"

28. Happy Halloween!! [image of jack-o'-lantern]

29. Have fun on Halloween today! [image of candy] [image of smiling face]

30. I hope you have a candyrific day today! [image of face with hearts in its eyes]

31. Happy Thanksgiving! [image of a turkey]

32. Sending you Thanksgiving love and kisses.

33. Thinking of you on Thanksgiving. So thankful for you! [image of heart]

34. Happy [winter holiday]! Sending love and presents your way. [image of present]

35. Hope you have a gift-filled, fun-packed, yummy food day today!

36. Memoji of you as a polar bear blowing kisses

37. Image of a dancer leaping with message "Happy Tutu Tuesday" (if your child likes to dance)

38. Happy pride month [image of pride]

39. Happy international pizza day [image of slice of pizza]

40. Happy first day of spring [image of flower]

Consideration

- Make sure that the holiday that you are commemorating is something that your child cares about or at least does not actively disdain because that would make your message seem really out of touch or provocative in a negative way.

Reflections

- *Are there certain holidays that are particularly joyful and meaningful for your child? How about for you?*

- *How can you acknowledge and celebrate the holiday in a meaningful and life-affirming way even if are separated from your child?*

- *If your child is not willing or able to accept a holiday greeting/ gift from you, are there other people in your life who would? How would it feel to focus your attention on them (e.g., volunteer at a soup kitchen on Thanksgiving)?*

TEN WAYS TO ASK "READ ANY GOOD BOOKS/SEEN ANY GOOD SHOWS LATELY?"

Purpose

As noted above, life goes on even though you are separated from your child and each of you are engaging in and participating in culture and popular culture. It is a fine topic of conversation to ask your child whether they have attended, participated in, or seen various events and activities, especially those that are highly likely to be of interest to your child. This is yet another way to show that you are thinking of them.

Examples

1. Seen any good movies lately?

2. Which season of [series] did you think was best?

3. Can you recommend a good psychological thriller to watch on [streaming service]?

4. If you were to recommend one book from [author], which would it be?

5. What is the best book you have read so far this year?

6. If you could see any musical theater show—past or present—which would it be?

7. Are there any songs that you are waiting to be dropped?

8. Have you been to any [sport] games lately?

9. What sports teams are you following these days?

10. What is a nice restaurant you have been to this year?

Considerations

- Make sure to be sensitive to your child's budget and lifestyle. If they are financially struggling, it might seem callous to ask them if they have been to a Broadway show lately or been out to eat.

- Make sure not to imply (unless you intend to) that you would take the child to see a game/show/etc.

Reflections

- *Are there certain activities and events that are particularly joyful and meaningful for your child? How about for you?*

- *How would it be for you to participate in the activity in a meaningful and life-affirming way even if are separated from your child?*

- *If your child is not willing or able to participate in this activity with you, who else in your life would? How would it feel to focus your attention on them (e.g., see a ballet with your niece rather than your child)?*

TEN WAYS TO MESSAGE A REQUEST FOR ADVICE

Purpose

Sometimes rejecting children will relate to a rejected parent if that parent asks them for advice, especially if it is on a topic that the child has specialized knowledge about (e.g., computers, cars, finances, video games, or Legos).

Examples

1. I'm thinking of buying a new computer for myself. What would you recommend?

2. I'd like to get [name of relative] a gift for graduation. Any thoughts?

3. [Your cousin Susie turned ten this week.] What's a good book for a ten-year-old girl?

4. What's the best pizza restaurant in town? I am craving some good old-fashioned pizza pie [image of pizza]

5. What's your opinion on [name] stock? I'm thinking of investing.

6. What are your thoughts about headphones? I need a pair for work and thought you might have some insight into which is best. [image of headphones]

7. I'm considering getting a new puppy. What are some breeds you particularly like? [image of puppy]

8. What's your take on the newest [model of car]? Grandma is thinking of getting one, and I thought you might want to weigh in on her decision.

9. Do you know anything about calligraphy? I was thinking of learning. Any tips?

10. I would love to hear your thoughts about [product/activity/location].

Considerations

- It is important not to pander to your child by elevating them beyond their actual knowledge level. In other words, if your child is a teenager with average knowledge about computers, it would not make sense to ask their opinion, especially because your child might feel insulted that you did not actually follow their suggestion. But you could share some of your own thoughts and inquire about theirs.

- Make sure not to ask advice about something that is a touchy subject. For example, if your child always wanted a certain expensive item related to their hobby and you did not purchase it for them but now you are asking their advice to purchase it for someone else, that would certainly hurt your child's feelings.

- Make sure not to imply that you are buying the object for them (unless you are, but then it would not be an advice message; it would be an offer to buy message).

Reflections

- *Does your child have specific talents, skills, and interests that you can reference in your message?*

- *What other ways can you find the help you are looking for if your child does not respond?*

- *How does it feel to ask your child for advice? Does it feel age appropriate, or does it feel like you are reinforcing the overempowerment of your child?*

- *Did your parents ask you for advice when you were the age your child is now; if so, how did it feel to you?*

TWENTY WAYS TO ASK ABOUT A PREFERENCE
Purpose
People, especially kids, usually have preferences for various things, such as TV shows, a sports team, a video game, a flavor of ice cream, or a pet cause. One way to feel close to a child is to get to know their preferences. That is why so many people ask children what their favorite color is or their favorite subject in school. It is possible that during the separation, your child's tastes have changed, so it could make sense to ask your child about what they are enjoying these days.

Examples
1. Just curious. What's your favorite ice cream flavor these days? [image of ice cream cone]

2. What's your favorite specialty drink this summer? [image of coffee]

3. Which is your favorite food right now [image of pizza] or [image of sushi] or something else?

4. If you had to choose: a lake or the ocean? [image of body of water]

5. What are your three favorite movies of all time? [image of movie tickets]

6. Which app are you using most: Instagram, Snapchat, TikTok, or some other app?

7. I am wondering if you are into graphic novels.

8. Where do you stand on [image of cat] versus [image of dog]?

9. Which subject are you enjoying the most this semester that you weren't sure that you would like?

10. If you could spend a day outside, what would you do?

11. Are you brand loyal to Apple or Samsung?

12. What dance class are you really enjoying these days? (for the dancer)

13. Are you favoring pop, rock, emo, or country these days?

14. Do you generally prefer to be inside or outside?

15. If you could visit anywhere in the world, where would you go?

16. Are you more into [image of football] or [image of soccer ball] nowadays?

17. Just wondering, what your favorite season is.

18. I have been wondering. What is one of your favorite holidays?

19. If you could play an instrument, what would it be?

20. If you were taking a trip, would you rather [image of train] or [image of boat]?

Considerations

- Some of these preferences can seem silly or trite, so you may want to be especially mindful of coming up with messages that are age appropriate.

- Try to avoid binary choices because that could reaffirm that it is okay to choose one thing over another (e.g., one parent over the other). Ideally, your child can love all of the important people in their life, and you don't want to suggest that most choices involve selecting one thing and discarding the other.

- Don't ask a child their preference for something that you should obviously know the answer to. For example, if your child has always loved dogs and plans to be a dog breeder, don't ask if your child prefers dogs over cats. You could ask which breed of dog your child is into or something more specific.

- Think about ways to build on the child's response—if you get one—so that the question does not seem so random. For example, if your child shares that they like basketball these days, you could then offer to go to a game together, or you could follow up and ask which teams they are following. If you don't follow up, it might seem as if you did not really care in the first place. So be sure to follow up with at least a response that acknowledges them.

Reflections

- *How would it feel to ask your child a question that in some respects highlights the distance between you, for instance, if you were more in touch with your child, you would probably know the answer and/or you would have other, more meaningful things to talk about?*

- *Can you think of these questions as conversation starters, just one more way to try to connect with your child?*

- *Try to think about your child as a specific individual and see what you are interested in learning about their tastes, interests, and preferences.*

- *How does it feel to know that other parents don't have to resort to such generic-seeming or even "forced" questions?*

- *What can you say to yourself to avoid shame, anger, bitterness, resentment, jealousy, and other negative emotions?*

Twenty Ways to Message a Thought-Provoking Question

Purpose

This kind of message is designed to provoke thought in the child, and it is far better than asking a mundane cliché question like "What did you do in school today?" This type of message probably works best for a situation in which there is some ongoing two-way communication. Otherwise, the question might seem too random and out of the blue.

Examples

1. What is the most interesting thing that happened to you today?

2. Did anything unexpected happen to you today?

3. What is something that took you by surprise?

4. Did anything interesting happen today?

5. What is the weirdest thing that happened to you this week?

6. What is the best thing that happened to you so far this year?

7. What took you by surprise today?

8. What is the oddest-looking animal you have ever seen?

9. What is the weirdest flavor of ice cream you have ever eaten?

10. What is the most interesting movie you have seen lately?

11. What celebrity do you find particularly interesting these days?

12. What was the most challenging homework assignment you had?

13. What is the last essay topic you had or chose to write about?

14. What movie were you really looking forward to that lived up to the promotional ads or your expectations?

15. What artist are you waiting for to drop a new song?

16. What game is most fun right now?

17. If you could create an app, what would it be?

18. What is a food you would like to try?

19. What is a book that you didn't think you would like but you really did?

20. If you had to describe yourself today in three words, what would they be?

Considerations

- You want to prepare yourself for the possibility that these kinds of questions could provoke an angry, hostile, or sarcastic response. For example, the child could respond "The weirdest thing is that you chose to text me," "Stop texting stupid questions," or "You don't get to ask me questions after what you did." Please refer below to "Ten Ways to Message an Invitation to Share" for suggestions about how to respond to these kinds of messages from the child.

- Make sure that your questions are age appropriate. For example, a ten-year-old might enjoy a question such as "If you were an animal, what animal would you be?" but most kids over that age would find that question extremely dull, irrelevant, or just corny. Take care in crafting your message to be appropriate to your targeted audience.

CHAPTER EIGHT

Reflections
- *Can you think of these questions as conversation starters, just one more way to try to connect with your child?*

- *Try to think about your child as a unique individual and see what you are interested in learning about your child's tastes, interests, and preferences.*

- *What can you say to yourself to avoid shame, anger, bitterness, resentment, jealousy, and other negative emotions?*

TEN WAYS TO MESSAGE AN INVITATION TO SHARE

Purpose

There may come a time when it makes sense to invite your child to share what is on their mind, especially in a way that is designed to provoke a response. It is very important—essential really—that you don't do this unless and until you are able to respond with loving compassion throughout the discussion as opposed to defensiveness, anger, or resentment.

Examples

1. I imagine you are pretty upset with me. I would like to hear about that.

2. I know that you are feeling hurt and angry with me right now. I am ready to listen.

3. I have lots of ideas about why you are mad at me but would love to hear directly from you what is bothering you.

4. Would you be willing to make a list of the reasons you are upset with me? I would really like to see that.

5. I want you to know that I am interested in hearing anything you would like to share with me.

6. I bet you are hurt and angry with me.

7. I have thought a lot about what is upsetting you. Can I share my ideas with you and see what you think?

8. I think you are feeling very hurt right now.

9. Your feelings really matter to me. I invite you to share whatever is on your mind.

10. I am all ears for anything you want to share with me.

Considerations

- Do not invite your child to share their thoughts and feelings with you unless you are ready to listen and not react in a negative way. You could set your relationship back considerably if your child takes you up on the offer and shares what is on their mind and then you respond in a way that shames or blames them or drifts into explanations and justifications. It is important just to listen. See Chapter 2 on what to do if your child responds with negativity and/or false allegations.

- Don't do this if your child already shared with you a long litany of their complaints.

- Don't add any cute emojis, memes, or images because it could dilute the intent of your offer.

Reflections

- *How do you feel when you think about inviting your child to share their thoughts and feelings with you?*

- *Are you worried that by inviting the child to focus on the negative that you will only make things worse?*

- *What do you need to feel ready to invite your child to share their thoughts and feelings with you?*

Responding to the Responses

PRINCIPLES OF RESPONDING

IT IS USUALLY A GOOD THING WHEN YOUR CHILD RESPONDS TO your message because they do not have to respond at all. With a few exceptions, *any* response is a positive. The exceptions are legal responses warning you that a restraining order has been taken out or your child's threats of self-harm if you continue to message. Short of that, any response from the child is hopeful in that it is the beginning or continuation of a dialogue. That doesn't mean it will feel good to receive an angry, rejecting message from your child. But those feelings can be mitigated by acknowledging to yourself that your child has opened up to you. Below are some basic guiding principles for how to respond.

Assume Your Messages Are Not Private

You don't know to whom your child will show your response, but you can bet that if your response is negative in any way, the other parent and perhaps others (e.g., therapists for the child, custody evaluators, mediators, judges, a spouse, and friends and family who can be persuaded that you are the problem) will be shown your message. Certainly, if you are involved in any legal disputes with the other parent, a nasty message from you will become part of the other side's case. Judges do not look kindly on parents being nasty or accusatory toward their children, and one nasty message from you could have as much weight in court as a whole string of bad acts on the part of the other parent. (This is, of course, unfair, but we have seen it happen too often to ignore.) You must always keep your side of the street clean so that there is no ammunition for the other side to use to muddy the waters and confuse the judge. The last thing you want is for the judge to conclude that "Well, both parties made mistakes, so there is no point in trying to rectify the situation."

Reflections
- *How do you feel when you think about your child sharing your messages with other people, especially people whom you feel have hurt you?*
- *What can you do with those feelings so they don't impede your ability to continue to reach out to your child?*
- *Do you feel ready to respond with compassion and interest instead of anger, sadness, or defensiveness?*

Connect, Don't Correct
You may feel a strong desire to correct your child if their response contains an accusation that is inaccurate. In general, corrective statements can feel like criticisms, and hence, they backfire. We believe that the best path forward is forged with love and compassion and that any response from your child can be met by you with an intent to connect (i.e., understand or show compassion for) rather than correct (i.e., tell them that they are wrong). In fact, it is our belief that correction occurs through connection. By this, we mean that if your child experiences you as safe, loving, and available through your emotionally connected communications, then your child's false belief about you will be corrected. Below are specific examples of how to respond when your child accuses you of something specific

that is untrue, but every response to your child should be seen through the lens of connection.

Reflections

- *How does it feel to hear that your child has misunderstandings about you that you cannot simply correct by sharing your perspective?*

- *Have you had the experience of someone trying to change your mind and its feeling insulting and out of touch with your thoughts and feelings?*

- *What do you need to be able to respond to your child without trying to change their mind?*

You Can Understand without Validating

Too often, rejected parents are instructed to "validate" their child's perspective and feelings even when the child seems to be mistaken. This can sometimes border on apologizing/admitting to something that you did not do, which can have far-reaching negative consequences. Validating can also sometimes involve apologizing for "anything I have done that hurt you," which generally lacks the specificity necessary for the recipient to feel satisfied. Instead of relying on the concept of validating—which could be unnecessarily agreeing with—the guiding principle we recommend is to show interest in and understanding of your child's thoughts and feelings. Rather than a false "If you think I hurt you, then I must have hurt you" or a generic "I am sorry for everything," we recommend that you try to *understand* the child's perspective, which is ultimately what all children want from their parents. This could mean restating the child's ideas to ensure that you understand, genuinely thanking the child for sharing, asking questions to gain a deeper understanding, and probing for what else the child wants you to understand about their experience. This can be thought of as "compassionate curiosity."

Reflections
- *Can you remind yourself that when in doubt, engage with compassionate curiosity?*
- *How does your child feel understood (e.g., verbal affirmations of "I understand" or by your asking questions to gain a deeper understanding, restating their ideas, or something else)?*
- *How can you resist the pressure to apologize for something you did not do?*

Build on What Your Child Says

Another principle when responding is to look at what your child is saying and really think about whether there is something there that you could or should be picking up on. For example, if the child tells you to stop sending gifts because they feel guilty, you can certainly ask about that feeling of guilt to try to understand where it is coming from. You can show interest in that idea by following up with a comment or question. Perhaps your child feels guilty because you are showering them with gifts while they are treating you so badly. Perhaps they feel guilty because they are getting all these gifts and their roommates are not. Perhaps there is an entirely different basis for the guilt. You won't know unless you ask. To not ask could make it seem as if you are not really interested. Another example would be if your child happens to mention a big test coming up, having a cold, or having a lot to do. Make sure to show interest in that by following up with expressions of concern, well-wishes, or questions to learn more.

SAMPLE RESPONSES

Here are some common and likely responses from a child to one of these texts and some suggested language for you to use in your response back. These proposed responses are designed to create a feeling of closeness and caring and to invite your child to share their experiences. Please keep in mind that you will probably have to work hard to maintain a position of loving connection and resist the urge to defend, deflect, explain, or justify.

Who Is This?

Your child might bluntly ask who the text is coming from. They may know that it is you and are sending this message to try to show you that you mean so little to them that you are not even in their contact list. This can feel very hurtful and rejecting. Try not to let the response sting so much, and bear in mind that your child did not have to text you at all. You cannot really know for sure why your child is asking, but it is recommended that you take this as a good sign because it is possibly an innocuous response and it does invite a response back. In this kind of situation, *any* response from your child is a good response because it creates an opening for a conversation. Your response should be straightforward.

Possible Responses
- "Your Mom"
- "It's your Dad, honey."
- Photo of you waving to your child

Considerations
- Avoid argumentative responses such as "You know who this is."
- Avoid self-serving or self-justifying responses such as "It is the woman who gave birth to you and took care of you your whole life"; "This is your dad, the person who has always been there for you"; or "I am the parent fighting to see their child."
- Avoid guilt-inducing or dramatic statements such as "I am desperate to be in touch with you" or "Why won't you see me?"

- Avoid statements that denigrate or blame someone else such as "I am the parent being kept from you" or "I am the parent you have been brainwashed against."
- Avoid maudlin or desperate statements such as "I am the parent who weeps for their lost child."

Why Are You Still Texting Me?

The implication of this question could be something like "You know I don't want you in my life, so why don't you just accept that and stop trying?" Of course, you cannot really know exactly what your child is trying to convey, but it is recommended that you take this as neither a positive nor a negative sign but rather see it as at least a little hopeful because it is a response and it does invite a response back. Moreover, your response back can address the underlying question being posed, which is, why are you still striving to have a relationship with them? Your response should treat this as a legitimate opportunity to share with the child how much they mean to you and how you will always want to have a better relationship.

Possible Responses
- "That is a great question! I am so glad you asked. I am texting because I love you."
- "Because you are important to me."
- "Because I will always hope to have a better relationship with you."
- "Because I want you to know that I am thinking about you even though we are not together right now."
- "Because our relationship matters to me."
- "Because you are always on my mind."

Considerations

- Avoid argumentative responses such as "How could you ask such a question!" or "You know why."

- Avoid self-serving responses such as "Because I am the kind of mother who will never stop trying to save her child."

- Avoid guilt-inducing or argumentative statements such as "If you weren't avoiding me, I wouldn't have to keep texting."

- Avoid statements that denigrate or blame someone else such as "Because you are being kept from me and the only way that I can reach you is by messaging."

- Avoid maudlin or desperate responses such as "Because what is a dad without his daughter?"

If You Keep Texting Me, I Am Going to Block You

It can feel very harsh to be on the receiving end of such a text. It has a harsh and aggressive tone and is threatening in nature. On the positive side, your child has not yet blocked you. Your response should be calm and loving, providing a clear message of your intent while acknowledging that the child has a right to block any number they want to.

Possible Responses

- "I think it is important for you to receive texts from me, but I understand that you might block me. I hope that you don't."

- "I think it is important for me to keep texting. You can respond to me with your feelings or any thoughts you are having."

- "I respect your privacy, but I was hoping that you would be interested in this subject."

- "I wish that you did not feel that way. I will try to limit my texts to other subjects."
- "Maybe there is some other way we can communicate?"

Considerations
- Avoid argumentative responses such as "If you do that, I will have to show up at your doorstep and try to talk sense into you."
- Avoid self-serving responses such as "You do what you have to do, and I will keep being a parent who is fighting for their child."
- Avoid guilt-inducing statements such as "I beg you not to cut me off!"
- Avoid statements that denigrate or blame someone else such as "Who gave you that idea?" or "You sound just like your [other parent/spouse, coach/etc.]."
- Avoid maudlin or desperate responses such as "Why would you do that to me?" or "I beg you not to block me."

If You Keep Texting Me, I Am Going to Get a Restraining Order
Like the response above, it can feel very harsh to be on the receiving end of such a text. It has a harsh and aggressive tone and is threatening in nature. On the positive side, your child has not yet taken a restraining order out on you. Your response should be calm and loving, providing a clear message of your intent to continue to reach out while acknowledging that the child has a right to try to take out a restraining order if they want to. It does probably make sense to reduce the frequency of texting and to offer that to show that you are hearing that your child is asking for you to stop.

Possible Response
- "I think it is important that you hear from me, so I am not going to stop all together. But I will certainly send fewer messages. I don't want to cause you stress and discomfort."
- "Is there something about this particular message that is upsetting for you?"

Considerations
- Avoid argumentative responses such as "No court would grant you a restraining order for this!"
- Avoid self-serving responses such as "You do what you have to do, and I will keep being a parent who is fighting for their child."
- Avoid guilt-inducing statements such as "If you would just agree to see me, I wouldn't have to keep texting."
- Avoid statements that denigrate or blame someone else such as "Who gave you that idea?" or "You sound just like your [other parent/spouse, coach/etc.]."
- Avoid maudlin or desperate responses such as "Why would you do that to me?" "I beg you not to do that to me," or "How could you be so cruel!"

You Never Cared Before, So Why Are You Acting Like You Care Now?

The child's response in this case is revealing that they feel abandoned, hurt, and rejected by you. It is actually very common for a child who is rejecting a parent to feel rejected by that parent. While it doesn't feel good to be accused of not caring, this is a hopeful response in that the child is revealing their feelings and that creates an opportunity for connection and reparation.

Possible Responses
- "I guess it seems like I am putting on a show that I care, but you are not buying it?"
- "You feel like I really missed some chances to show that I love you?"
- "Do you think I am texting just to look like I care but I don't really?"
- "Something isn't ringing true about my texts?"
- "It feels like I am being a phony?"
- "I am so sorry that you don't feel that I care. I would like to find a way to show you that I do."
- "It must hurt to feel that I never cared before!"
- "Would you share some ways that you feel that I failed to show that I cared? I would really like to understand your experience."
- "Can you say more about that?"
- "Thank you for letting me know that you feel that I don't care. That must hurt, and I am sorry that I caused you pain. I know in my heart that I care, but I hear that it doesn't feel that way to you."

Considerations
- Avoid argumentative responses such as "Well, I actually care very much, and you know that!"
- Avoid self-serving responses such as "I care more than most moms/dads who would probably not put up with what I put up with just to have a relationship with you."
- Avoid guilt-inducing statements such as "After everything I have done, you still don't think I care?"
- Avoid statements that denigrate or blame someone else such as "I think someone put that idea in your head. That doesn't sound like you."

- Avoid maudlin or desperate responses such as "I have cared for you since the day you were born, and I will never stop caring, no matter what anyone says."

Your Messages Are Stupid

Since your child does not have to respond at all, this kind of cheap-shot response can be viewed as a way for your child to maintain contact—even though the content is negative. Responses should focus on the positive rather than your hurt or angry feelings.

Possible Responses

- "Any message in particular?"
- "Stupid how? Too babyish or something else?"
- "Thanks for letting me know. I am still getting the hang of messaging." [image of chagrined emoji]
- "Thanks for letting me know. Any advice about how to message better?"
- "Any tips for improving my messaging? I'm all ears."
- "Suggestions for improvement?"
- "Care to elaborate?"
- "Any topic in particular?"
- "Too many emojis?"
- "I would love to be a better texter. Any suggestions?"
- "What are your top three pieces of advice for me?"
- "Really? I thought I was doing okay." [image of surprised emoji]
- "Well, that's a bummer for you. How can I do better?"
- "Any suggestions for a smart (and loving) message?"

Considerations
- Respond with an open mind to all criticism. If you can engage your child in a conversation about messages—even if the focus is on what you are doing wrong—it is still a positive because you are *relating* about something real.
- Avoid argumentative responses such as "Well, you don't have to be cruel. At least I'm trying."
- Avoid self-serving responses such as "I don't know any other parent who tries harder than I do!"
- Avoid guilt-inducing statements such as "No matter how hard I try, it's never good enough, is it?"
- Avoid statements that denigrate or blame someone else such as "I guess your [other parent/spouse/coach/etc.] sends just the best messages!" (Resentment only makes it worse.)
- Avoid maudlin or desperate responses such as "Isn't it ever good enough? Why can't you see how hard I am trying?"

If You Really Cared, You Would Know the Answer to Your Questions

This kind of response from your child would likely be in response to a text from you asking questions about your child's preferences. This response reveals that the child is hurt that you are asking questions that reveal you are out of step with who they are now. You can channel that empathy for your child in your response.

Possible Responses
- "I can see how it could look that way to you. I know in my heart I care about you, but I understand that my text is showing that I am out of touch with your life right now."
- "I'm sorry that it hurts that I don't know the answers already."
- "Is it possible that I care *and* I don't know the answer?"

- "I know in my heart that I care, but I hear you that it doesn't feel that way to you."
- "I see that it seems like I don't care. I know that I do and will work harder to show it in my messages."
- "I will try to ask better questions."
- "I am sorry that you feel that I don't care. Is there another way that I can show you that I do care?"
- "I wish that I knew the answers to these questions."

Considerations
- Avoid argumentative responses such as "Of course, I care" or "Why would you say I don't care?"
- Avoid self-serving responses such as "If only you knew how much I care!" or "It's not my fault I don't know these things anymore."
- Avoid guilt-inducing responses such as "Actually, I am the parent who really cares about you."
- Avoid statements that denigrate or blame the other parent such as "Your [other parent] didn't even know the name of your school until third grade, but I'm the parent who you think doesn't know you?"
- Avoid maudlin or desperate responses such as "Can't you see how hard I am trying?"

It's Too Late; I've Given You Too Many Chances Already
Possible Responses
- "I will keep trying even though you feel you have given me too many chances."
- "I am holding on to the belief that it is never too late to try to repair our relationship."
- "What can I do or say to make our communication feel better?"

Considerations
- Avoid argumentative responses such as "Who are you to say how many chances I deserve?" or "Why do you have to doubt everything I do and say?"
- Avoid self-serving responses such as "I'm your parent and I deserve another chance, especially after everything I have done for you."
- Avoid guilt-inducing responses such as "Do you know how much it hurts to hear you say that?"
- Avoid statements that denigrate or blame the other parent such as "Look at what your [other parent] has done, and you haven't cut them off."
- Avoid maudlin or desperate responses such as "Just tell me what to do and I will do it" or "Can't you see how hard I am trying? Don't I get any credit for that?"

SPECIFIC COMPLAINT THAT IS NOT TRUE

One of the most challenging aspects of relating to a hurt, angry, rejecting, distant child is when the child accuses the parent of doing something that the parent feels is mostly if not entirely untrue. As noted above, the problem for the parent is that the logical and rational response is to say some version of "that's not true." However, that does not work, especially if the parent responds with "That's ridiculous! Why would you believe that?" or "That's a lie! You know that's not true." While it seems logical to want to explain to your child that they are wrong for thinking you did this terrible thing that you did not do, that does not work. That is because if you say to your child "That's ridiculous," you are basically calling your child a fool or an idiot for believing something like that and therefore, you are insulting your child. If you tell your child that they know something isn't true or that something is a lie, then you are calling your child a liar. Since calling a child a liar or an idiot is hostile and rude, it will only exacerbate the situation, so you want to avoid responses like that. Moreover, if you respond with hurtful responses like that you are probably reinforcing the negative idea of who you are.

What could be helpful in this situation is the five steps. The full five steps are explained and demonstrated in Chapter 2, so the focus here is on modifying them for text messaging purposes.

For step one, gratitude, you may want to make it brief and simply say "Thank you for sharing this with me. I always want to know if you are feeling upset with me." You could add a heart emoji or a picture that connotes gratitude. Remember that you want your child to walk away from the experience feeling good about themselves and you.

For step two, compassion, you will not have access to all four sources of information (i.e., words, tone of voice, facial expression, and body posture), but you may be able to discern what your child is feeling from words and any emojis and italics that they are using in their message. For a text message, you might want to simply say "I sense that you are feeling quite upset with me about that. If we were together, I would try to figure out whether you are feeling angry, hurt, scared, worried, or confused." Of course, the word "sense" only makes sense if your child has not explicitly said what they are feeling. If your child texted that they are furious with you because they think that you did something and then you respond with a statement that says that you sense they are upset, it would seem bizarre and reinforce the idea you don't care and that you did not even bother to read their text and take in what they were saying.

Step three, empathy, is designed to show your child that you are trying to look at the situation from their point of view. This does not mean that you necessarily agree or disagree with your child. Using the same scenario as before, here is what it would sound like: "If I believed what you believe, I would probably be feeling what you were feeling. I get where you are coming from."

Step four is the minor correction, which is your chance to share with your child your perspective. Refresh your memory of the different versions (see Chapter 2) depending on whether the complaint is subjective or objective and whether it involves a third party. Since this step is already only one sentence, there is no need to modify it for text messaging purposes.

Step five is a recap of the first three steps. For texting purposes, you could say "I understand that this is how it seems to you. I am so grateful that you are letting me know."

If the accusation is relevant for the future, not just the past, such as "You don't listen to me" and there could be multiple opportunities to listen going forward, you could still end the text message version of the five steps with an invitation such as "I invite you to tell me any time that you feel that I'm not listening, and I will stop what I'm doing and focus more on trying to understand what you're saying." If the accusation is that you yell, you could say "I invite you to tell me any time that you feel that my tone of voice is too loud or intense, and I will speak more quietly."

Reflections

- *Can you imagine yourself using the five steps? What do you need to do to feel comfortable with using them? Would it help to practice?*

- *What are some false accusations your child is likely to bring up? Would it help to prepare yourself by making a list so that you are not taken by surprise? Does it help you feel more compassionate to think that your child is hurt by you rather than trying to hurt you?*

- *How can you give up your need to have your child know your side of the story?*

SPECIFIC COMPLAINT THAT IS MOSTLY TRUE

Also, as noted above, if the child's accusation is at least partly true, you don't want to spend fifteen sentences going through the first three steps. That is just too long for the child to wait for you to acknowledge that you see the situation the same way they do. A modified five steps is in order. Because the first three steps (i.e., gratitude, compassion, and empathy) are already shortened, there is no additional modification necessary for doing this process via text as opposed to in person or on the phone.

Step one as a text would be something like "Thank you so much for telling me that you are thinking about my having slapped you when you were ten years old."

Step two as a text could be "I can see how upset it's making you." If the child is sharing an actual feeling in their text to you, reference that specific feeling (e.g., anger, sadness, fear, or confusion).

Step three in a text would be something like "If I were a [age] kid and I was remembering a time when my [parent] slapped me when I was ten, I might be pretty [insert emotion] too."

Step four would not be a correction. Instead, you would want to acknowledge the event, saying "You know, I remember it the same way you do." Then you would apologize: "I am so sorry that I did that." After you acknowledge and apologize, you can add some questions engaging in "compassionate curiosity" to show your child that you are interested in their felt experience and that you are not afraid to go deeper into the child's pain. You ask questions because you care. You can then end the modified five steps with a wish such as "If I could go back in time, I would do things differently"; "I wish that I had not done that"; or "If I could do things over again, I would always show you love and respect even when we are not seeing eye-to-eye." Remember that at no point should you explain your side of the story, justify what you did, or minimize its impact on your child.

Reflections

- *How would it feel for you to respond to your child's complaint without trying to share your perspective?*
- *Have you had the experience of someone apologizing but then minimizing, explaining, or justifying? How did that feel to you?*

- *What are some complaints that have at least some truth to them that your child is likely to bring up? Would it help to prepare yourself by making a list so that you are not taken by surprise? Does it help you feel more compassionate to think that your child is hurt by you rather than trying to hurt you?*

CLOSING THOUGHTS

Having a hurt, angry, rejecting, distant child is one of the most painful experiences any parent can go through, and our hearts are with you. In Part II of this book, we offer a general approach as well as hundreds of specific suggestions for sending messages to your child to help inspire, motivate, and guide you along the way. It is our greatest hope that these suggestions are helpful to you. If your hurt, angry, rejecting, distant child is now an adult, it might make sense to reach out to them with a carefully crafted letter designed to reignite the spark of connection that lies within the child, such as the one described briefly in Baker and Fine (2014b) and expanded on in Part III of this book.

Reflections

- *Do you feel inspired and motivated to keep sending messages to your child?*
- *If not, what additional support and guidance might you need?*
- *We invite you to hold in your heart the value of your relationship with your child.*
- *We invite you to remind yourself every day that your child needs to experience you as safe, loving, and available and that those qualities need to be reflected in everything you do and say.*

Part III

How to Communicate by Letter with a Hurt, Angry, Rejecting, Distant Child

IF YOUR HURT, ANGRY, REJECTING, DISTANT CHILD IS OVER EIGH-teen and texting has not yet generated a significant improvement in the relationship, then it is time to think about writing a letter to them, especially if they live away from home. An earlier version of the letter is briefly described in *Surviving Parental Alienation: A Journey of Hope and Healing* (Baker & Fine, 2014b), but we have learned so much since then about how to explain the philosophy of the letter as well as the various components. This letter, by the way, is designed to be written from a parent to an adult child. It could—with some modification—be used to write to a daughter- or son-in-law or even a sibling or friend. However, the version presented here is the version for parent to child. This part of the book presents the philosophy of the letter, homework in prepara-tion for the letter, the components of the letter with examples, ideas about how to respond to the child's response to the letter, and some possible next steps. This portion of the book is relevant for children from teenage years through adulthood and is primarily relevant for situations in which there is a total or near-total cut off with the hurt, angry, rejecting, distant child.

Chapter Ten

Philosophy of the Letter

The Focus Is on the Child's Point of View

In beginning to think about writing a letter to your adult child, it may help to close your eyes and take a few deep breaths. Imagine that you are standing on the bank of a turbulent river and your adult child is on the other side. The river itself represents all the hurt and anger that lie between you and your hurt, angry, rejecting, distant child. If you are like many other parents of an adult hurt, angry, rejecting, distant child, you have done numerous things over the years to reach out to them. Perhaps you have told your child that you are sorry for everything they think you did that hurt them. Perhaps you have pleaded with them to understand that there are two sides to every story and that if they understood your side of the story, they would not be so angry with you. But these efforts have fallen on deaf ears because—in keeping with our metaphor of the river—that is like standing on your side of the river asking your child to come to your side and look at the relationship from your point of view. That generally does not work. It's like yelling into the wind; your voice gets drowned out by the rushing sound of the water and air. If your child has cut you off, they are very hurt and angry, and at this time are not motivated to do the hard work of trying to see things from your perspective.

As an alternative, we offer this method for writing a letter, which—in keeping with the metaphor—involves you, the parent, building a bridge, walking across that bridge and standing next to your adult son or daughter, and looking back at the relationship from their point of view.

Reflections

- *What comes to your mind when you think about your child standing on the other side of the river?*
- *What do you feel in your heart when you imagine the river?*
- *What worries come to mind when you think about building this bridge?*

SOME WORRIES YOU MIGHT HAVE

In thinking about this idea of your building a bridge, a couple of concerns might come to mind. You might be thinking "Why should I apologize for something I did not do?"; "I already tried that, and it didn't work"; or "I am the victim here. Why should I be chasing my child?" Each of these concerns will be addressed. Even if you are not aware of having these concerns, it is still important to hear our responses because they are part of explaining the thought process underlying the letter.

First, at no point does the letter involve your apologizing for something you did not do. Sometimes parents in your situation get trapped in a binary thought process that says you either prove you didn't do something (i.e., prove your innocence) or apologize for something you did not do (i.e., admit that you are guilty). But rest assured that there is a middle space that involves acknowledging your child's perspective without agreeing with it or arguing about the facts. This will be explained further below.

Reflections

- *What worries do you have when thinking about writing the letter?*

- *Can you imagine finding a way to communicate that does not involve proving your innocence or admitting to your guilt?*

- *Can you set aside this concern until you know more about the letter?*

The second concern that you might have is that you have already written a letter like the one recommended here and it did not work, so why bother writing another letter. This is possible. However, it is also possible that the letters you have written—even if based on the template in a prior book or on advice from someone else—might not have included all the necessary elements as outlined here or they did not fully embody the philosophy of the proposed letter. Looking at letters that other parents have written, it seems that these letters tend to include the parent's explanation of their side of the story because it can be very difficult to avoid doing so. There is a rational notion that if your child is hurt and angry with you because they think something about you that is not true or that fails to consider some essential context, then the solution to resolving their anger and hurt is to explain that it did not happen or did not happen in the way that they think it did. The approach of the letter being described here is that it does not include any aspect of explaining, justifying, or minimizing. There is a time and a place for that but not in this letter. While it is possible that you have already written a letter exactly like what is being recommended, it is more likely that previous letters have not quite followed the template and approach recommended here. We want to be clear that it is very difficult to stay true to the philosophy and intent of the letter. The letter requires that you avoid inserting your perspective (explanations, justifications), something that is very hard to do. Therefore, we recommend strongly that you write the letter with a mental health professional or trusted friend familiar with the proposed approach to help you stay on the other side of the river. The last thing you want to do is send a letter that inadvertently reinforces the negative idea of who you are, so we encourage you to have someone else work with you on this process.

Reflections

- *Do you feel that you have already tried writing a letter and it did not work?*

- *Can you hold onto the idea that there might be a different way to write a letter than what you have already tried?*

- *Can you set aside your doubt until you know more about the letter?*

The third concern some parents have is that it is unfair for them to have to do this really hard work of building the bridge because they have already been so maligned and mistreated and lost precious time with their child. And that is true! Of course, no one should write the letter unless they want to. However, there are some reasons why you, the parent, may choose to write the letter even though it is unfair. First, you are the parent, and parents generally must make the greater effort in the parent–child relationship because that is its nature. Second, you are older and wiser and have more life experience, so it is fitting for you to do this work. And third, you are the person who is most in touch with the desire to repair the relationship. Research and clinical practice strongly support the belief that most adult children—even those who are very hurt, angry, rejecting, and distant—want a relationship with the parent they have rejected but that desire is sometimes buried and repressed. Between the two of you, you are the person who is more aware of and filled with yearning to improve your relationship with your child. Thus, you are the one who will probably need to take the first step and write the letter.

Reflections
- *Can you relate to the idea that it is unfair for you to be in the situation that you are in?*
- *Can you hold onto the hope that your child wants a relationship with you even though they are currently actively rejecting you?*
- *Can you set aside your feelings of injustice so that you can open your heart to your child?*

Of course, you can keep doing what you are doing, or you can decide to try something new. It is entirely your choice. The letter represents one possible next step, which you get to decide if that works for you.

As noted in Chapter 5, under the heading "Why You Should Message Your Child Even Though You May Not Get a Response," the parent in the book *The Runaway Bunny* can provide an excellent guiding example for you as you write your letter to your hurt, angry, rejecting, distant child. Recall that in the book, the baby bunny imagines various scenarios of running away, such as joining the circus or becoming a crocus in a hidden flower garden, a bird that flies away, or a boat that sails away. In response, the mother never gets her feelings hurt or gets angry. She always responds with a loving message such as "If you become a bird and fly away from me, I will become a tree that you come home to"; "If you join the circus and become a trapeze artist, I will become a tightrope walker and I will walk across the air to you"; or "If you become a little boy and run into a house, I will become a mother and catch you in my arms and hug you." In the end, the little bunny decides he might as well be her little bunny. This mother bunny is a role model and a shining example of how you can remain calm and loving and not feel offended by your child's desire for separation and independence. She maintains an unwavering positive image of her role in her child's life; therefore, she can respond to his rejection in a loving and connected manner. This mother bunny can hold in her heart the value that her relationship with her child has. Many parents of children who are hurt, angry, rejecting, and distant receive messages from the child, the other parent, a daughter-in-law or son-in-law, the legal system, mental health professionals, and even friends and family that they are not important. The child might be saying "I've already replaced you," "You were never that important to me," or "There's no role for you in my life." People might be encouraging you to give up and move on, that your kids don't really need you. We don't believe that's true.

We believe that even when a child is rejecting a parent, that child wants a relationship with the parent whom they are rejecting. In research with adult children who were turned against a parent by the other parent when they were children, it is clear that the rejecting child does not fully intend to cut that parent out of their life even if the words on the page in a letter they write to the parent or the words they say in person, on the phone, or to a therapist about that parent indicate a complete and utter lack of interest in the relationship (Baker, 2007). Even when the child messages an unambiguous statement that they do not want a relationship with that parent, it turns out in many cases that the child does want a relationship. The presentation of extreme and utter lack of investment in the relationship is a false presentation much of the time. It's very hard as the person on the receiving end of an absolute statement of rejection to hold on to the idea that your child does not mean everything they say. Now to be clear, you cannot tell the child "Oh, you don't really mean that. That's not how you really feel" because that would be insulting to the child. But you can hold in your heart and mind the belief that the child's rejection is probably not as absolute as they are presenting it to be.

We believe that that relationship has value and meaning even if other people are not able to honor that value in the moment. It is your job as the parent to honor that value and hold it in your heart. We invite you to channel your inner mother bunny (or father bunny) when thinking about writing this letter.

Reflections
- *Can you hold in your heart the value and meaning that your relationship with your child has even while others may be invalidating your value to the child?*

- *Do you relate to the mother bunny from the book, or is there another role model of parental acceptance that is more motivating and inspiring for you?*

- *What do you need to do to find the strength to forge on despite the obstacles that you face?*

Returning to the notion of the bridge, we want to be clear that it must be forged from the love that you have for your child and the belief that they still love you even if they cannot admit it right now. You must make this effort with love and compassion—not resentment—in your heart. The bridge is not a demand or expectation for an apology from the child. It is not a demand that they see and know your side of the story. It is not an expectation that the child will see anyone else the same way that you do. (There may never be a fully shared understanding of what happened.) It also does not involve groveling and insincere contrition by you for crimes you did not commit (i.e., false dichotomy). There is another way to respond to a hurt, angry, rejecting, distant child.

Reflections
- *How does it feel to think that you and your child may never have a shared perspective about your relationship?*

- *What would it mean to you if your child never apologized for the ways in which they have hurt you?*

We now return to the notion of finding a space that neither demands your child see things from your point of view (i.e., proving you are innocent) nor agrees with the child's false narrative (i.e., admitting your guilt). The story of a former client is offered to illustrate what this means in a practical sense. This client shared that when her son was seven years old, she asked the father if she could move away with their son, and according to her, he agreed. So she sold her house, quit her job, and got a new house and a new job several states away. The day before she was set to move, the father filed an emergency motion preventing her from taking the boy with her. She lost the temporary hearing and decided to move anyway, without her son, hoping that she would win at the trial. However, she did not win at the trial, and she was never the primary caregiver again. According to her, she and her son eventually became cut off from each other. By the time she came to me, she had already reached out to him and written him several letters explaining that it was not her fault that she lived so far away. She shared that his father had tricked her into moving away and that she suffered from missing him. Her efforts did not succeed in repairing the relationship.

This was not surprising since her efforts at that point had involved explaining to her son that he was wrong or stupid for feeling the way that he did. So she was helped to write a letter (similar to the one described in this part of the book). In her letter, one paragraph addressed the issue that she had moved away. This parent did not want to grovel; she did not want to admit that she had abandoned her son, nor did she want to argue with him. The paragraph sounded something like this: "I imagine that you are hurt and angry that I moved five hundred miles away. You were just a little boy of seven years of age. You were used to seeing your mom and dad every week, and then all of a sudden, your mom was an airplane ride away, and you only saw me on holidays and the summer. What a big change for such a little boy." At this point in the paragraph, she was writing about the experience from the child's point of view. Then she continued by asking questions not to make him justify his feelings but to show deep interest in his felt experience. She wrote, "What was that like for you? Were there times that you missed me and needed me to be there for you and I wasn't? Did other kids tease you because they lived with their moms and you didn't? Did you feel that if I really loved you, I would not have moved away?" And then she ended the paragraph with a wish about something she could have done differently: "I wish I had worked harder at the time to understand what it felt like for you when I moved away." It is our belief that healing could occur because this mother made the effort to understand her son's lived experience and demonstrated her deep interest in his perspective. By asking these types of questions, the mother was showing her son that she could tolerate his perspective and wanted to hold his pain.

Reflections

- *Did you have an emotional response in reading this mother's efforts to see the situation from her child's point of view?*

- *Do you feel excited by the idea that there is a way to acknowledge your child's perspective that does not involve groveling and false contrition on your part?*

- *What worries come to mind when you think about trying to write such a letter to your child?*

To recap, the bridge represents a heartfelt effort to see the relationship from your child's point of view. It involves standing on the banks of the other side of the river and looking at the relationship from your child's perspective. The letter provides an important opportunity for you to show yourself to be safe, loving, and available so you can counter the distorted messages about you. It also provides you with the opportunity to expand your own awareness of the relationship from the child's point of view. This can create a greater capacity for you to respond to your child in a way that will affirm the relationship. And the letter can create a paradigm shift within you that can affect how you think and feel about your child. The letter represents an opportunity to induce greater compassion within you for your child's suffering. If this philosophy resonates with you, then we invite you to proceed to the next chapter, where the preparatory work is described.

Homework for the Letter

IN PREPARATION FOR WRITING THE LETTER, THERE ARE THREE pieces of homework that you can do. The first piece of homework requires some explanation. So let's begin with you imagining that your adult child makes a new friend. Perhaps this friend is their roommate in college, a colleague at work, or an old friend with whom they have become reacquainted. After a while, this new friend asks your adult child why they are hurt, angry, rejecting, and distant from you. There are five possible responses to this question that your child could but most likely would not say. The first is "Well, my other parent [or some other third party] engaged in the seventeen primary parental alienation strategies and fostered my unjustified rejection of that parent." The second is "The reason I am so hurt, angry, rejecting, and distant is that I am a terrible person and I just want to break that parent's heart." The third is "I'm psychotic and my behavior has no relationship to reality." The fourth is "My parent slurps their soup (or some other frivolous complaint), and therefore, I cannot have them in my life." And the final thing your child could but would not say is "You know, I just don't remember." The reason your child will not say any of these things is that they are a human being. All human beings, with the exception perhaps of sociopaths, want to see themselves as good and rational people and believe that a good person does not cut off a parent for slurping their soup or for no reason at all.

A rational person would not cut off a parent knowing they've been manipulated to do so but still choosing not to have a relationship. The question remains then regarding what your adult child would say in response to the question of why they are so hurt, angry, rejecting, and distant from you.

Most likely, your child would offer to this new friend plausible-sounding grievances. It used to be thought that if a child were being manipulated to reject a parent, the person doing the manipulating would fabricate a criticism of the parent and then convince the child that it was true to get the child to be hurt, angry, and rejecting of that parent. But now we understand that it's much more effective and common for a person to refer to things that the to-be rejected parent actually did and that the child actually has feelings about and then to amplify the child's hurt and anger about those things. What the person can do is convince the child that because you did that behavior, you are unsafe, unloving, and unavailable. And it resonates for the child because they have their own feelings of frustration, hurt, or anger about whatever you really did. The point is that your child would offer plausible-sounding reasons for their being so hurt, angry, rejecting, and distant, and if you want to try to repair the relationship, the first step is to think about what your child's grievances are.

For that reason, your first piece of homework is to think about what your child would say are the reasons they are hurt, angry, rejecting, and distant with you and then to make a list of those reasons. You can think about this exercise as your first opportunity to walk across that bridge and look at the relationship from the child's perspective as if you're watching a movie of their childhood, but it's the child version of the movie, not your version. At this point, you are not actually writing the letter; you are just writing a list. The list should sound like it was written by the child so that if you are the mother and your child thinks that you had an affair and ruined the family, the first item on the list might be "She had an affair and ruined the family." If you are the father and you think that your child would say that you yelled all the time and favored their brother, then the first item on your list might be "He favored my brother," and the second item might be "He yelled at me all the time." You're going to put the items on this list in the child's voice. Bear in mind that for some of the things on the list, there might be no truth, a little truth, or a lot of truth. Your job in making the list is to let go of the worry that some things on the list do not match your memory and your understanding of what happened. Just make the list of what you think your child would say in response to the question of why they are so hurt, angry, rejecting, and distant from you. The mother who moved away (in the story told earlier) would put on her list "My mother abandoned me" because that is her understanding of her son's experience. She was not comfortable with the word "abandon" and it did not end up in her actual letter, but the starting point for her was to understand that this was how her son felt. You should aim to have ten to fifteen items on the list. It does not need to be so detailed such as "They made me eat broccoli on Monday" and then "They made me eat broccoli on Tuesday." You do not need to drill down quite that much. It could say "They didn't listen to me and made me eat food I didn't like." That would be at the correct level of specificity.

Being stuck and not being able to think of what to put on the list probably means that you need to spend more time thinking about walking across that bridge and really pondering your child's perspective. And if you make the list too quickly assuming that you know all of their complaints and grievances, you might be rushing and thereby missing something of importance to your child. Make sure to take your time. Of course, if your child has sent you a letter or email telling you many or all of the things they're upset about, you should refresh your memory by rereading that letter or email even though it's probably very painful to do so.

As a way to get you started in this process, you might also want to think about categories of potential grievances such as issues related to money; for example, did you refuse to pay for something that the child believes you should have paid for, whether it's horseback riding lessons or college or whatever? For children, money represents love. So if a parent does not pay for something or the child thinks the parent has not or will not pay for something, that could be on the list because to the child, it could feel like you don't really care. There are often issues of favoritism. Perhaps your child feels that you prefer one of the other children in the family over them. Or conversely, perhaps your child feels that you have been harsh or unkind toward a sibling and they feel upset about that. Often, which parent ended the marriage and which parent moved out of the home could be subjects relevant to your child. It may seem to the child that you cared more about yourself than the family. Children often have grievances around feeling accepted by a parent. For example, if your child wanted to study art and felt that you minimized that and steered them toward a career in science instead, that could be a source of grievance. Issues of feeling accepted are particularly relevant for children who are not cisgender (i.e., they are non-binary, transgender, or gay). It is important that you really think about this homework and what is hurting your child and where your child feels wounded by the relationship.

EXAMPLES TO FOLLOW THE PHRASE "I AM HURT, ANGRY, REJECTING, AND DISTANT FROM [MOTHER/FATHER] BECAUSE . . ."

- they are a liar and cannot be trusted.
- they broke up the family and cared more about themselves than the family.
- they were mean to my [other parent], which made their life harder.
- they focused more on work and travel than on taking care of the family.
- they violated my boundaries and privacy by coming into my room without knocking, looking into my private stuff,

snooping around, and asking embarrassing questions of me and my friends.

- they acted weird, dressed oddly, looked weird, and embarrassed me at school and in the community.
- they tried to act too young, which embarrassed me, and tried to be my friend instead of a parent.
- they were angry all the time, yelled at me and my siblings, called us names, and were mean.
- they were in a bad mood a lot, slamming doors and being cranky, which made the home unpleasant.
- they didn't accept me for who I am, wanted me to be something I am not, and didn't listen to what I wanted.
- they didn't pay for college/dance lessons/private school even though they had the money.

Reflections
- *What does it feel like to think about your child's grievances from their point of view?*
- *What feelings get generated when you think about your child's grievances?*
- *Can you make your list without inserting your perspective?*

The second piece of homework requires you to think; you don't have to write anything down until you're working on the letter. The task is to think about something fun you did with your child when they were much younger that had a pleasant aroma attached to it. Examples might be baking chocolate chip cookies with your child. That's a fun thing to do for most kids, because they like to stir in the ingredients, mix the dough, and eat the cookies, and the activity has a pleasant aroma associated with it. The whole house smells like chocolate, butter, and sugar while the cookies are baking. Another example might be going to a favorite bakery or pizza parlor with your child. As you walk into one of those places, you are instantly surrounded by a very lovely aroma, and it's fun to be out for dinner. Maybe your child liked to go to that bakery and pick out cupcakes to bring home to the family. Other ideas that are not food related could be giving a puppy a bubble bath that smelled good. Playing with Play-Doh could be relevant if your child liked its smell. Horseback riding would work if that was fun for the child and they enjoyed the smell of the hay, the leather, and the horses. Other ideas include campfires and going to the movies (because when you walk into a movie theater you immediately smell popcorn). Going to the beach can also be included if your child enjoyed that because the salty air has a distinct aroma and there are usually olfactory associations with sunblock and perhaps popsicles or other snacks eaten there. You only need to think of one thing that you did with your child when they were younger that was associated with a pleasant smell. Activities that would be less helpful for this task include skiing and any other outdoor winter sport because there may not have been enough of a sensory component associated with it. Also, going to the zoo might not work because although it is usually fun for children to go to the zoo, the aroma is often unpleasant. Also, don't include something that could have been fun and definitely had a good aroma but for some reason you did not actually have a good time.

Reflections

- *How does it feel to spend time remembering positive moments with your child?*
- *What self-care would be helpful as you think about positive memories you have of a better time with your child?*
- *What do you feel in your heart when you think about those better times?*

The third piece of homework is to find an attractive photograph of your child when they were about five years old. The picture shouldn't be of them crying, scowling, or showing an unflattering facial expression. It should also not be a photograph of your child hugging you because the purpose is not to prove to your child that they used to like you. There's a different purpose, which becomes clear once the letter is being written, but for homework purposes, the goal is just to find an attractive photograph of your five-year-old child, ideally, alone.

As a word of caution, you might feel sad while doing the homework because it involves thinking about your child's grievances or even reading their letters of complaint, which can be very painful. It also involves going down memory lane and thinking about fun things that you did together, which can be painful. And you will be looking through photographs and remembering a time when your child was so dear and innocent and less hurt, angry, rejecting, and distant. Try to schedule time do that homework, which allows you the opportunity to feel your feelings and try to remain hopeful that by working on the letter, you are doing something constructive to repair the relationship.

Reflections

- *What comes to mind when you look at photos of the five-year-old version of your child?*

- *What do you feel in your heart when you look at those pictures?*

- *What can you do to help yourself if you feel flooded with sadness, grief, or other painful emotions?*

Chapter Twelve

Components of the Letter

IN THIS CHAPTER, WE WILL EXPLAIN THE DIFFERENT ELEMENTS of the letter and the purpose of each, provide a few examples, and offer some considerations.

THE GREETING

Explanation

You want to open the letter with a warm and loving greeting to signal from the outset that the letter is a safe place for your child to be devoting their attention. Open your heart to your child by creating a warm and loving greeting. Imagine that you are standing before the best version of your child and speaking to them.

Examples

- My darling daughter
- My sweet son
- To my dear [name or nickname]
- Dearest [name or nickname]

Considerations

If your child has decided to adopt a new name as part of a gender transition or for some other reason, it would probably make sense to use that preferred name rather than the name that was given to your child at birth. It can sometimes feel unsettling or like a concession to use the child's new name, especially if you feel that the gender transition and/or adoption of the new name was part of someone else's manipulation to control the child. However, refusing to use the name could feel to the child as if you are not accepting them and listening to them and could create so much resentment that the child will not be receptive to anything else you say in the letter. It is possible, of course, to simply not use the child's name at all in the greeting, which buys you some time to address the issue at a later date.

Reflections

- *Is your heart open to your child as you begin the process of writing the letter?*

- *What is the warmest opening you can come up with to show your child that you are coming from a place of love and acceptance?*

- *Is this the right time to write the letter? How would you know if it is not the right time?*

ACKNOWLEDGE THE DISTANCE

Explanation

The first paragraph of the letter is designed to show your child from the outset that you are willing to be honest about the difficulties in the relationship. You are signaling that you can be honest about what is happening and that you have the intention to address some hard truths in the letter. The paragraph also contains a description of an early attachment memory, hopefully to create a feeling of warmth and love between you and your child, the reader of the letter.

Examples

- I have been thinking a lot lately about the distance in our relationship. I know that it has been a long time since we have been close. When I held you in my arms for the first time and saw your little button nose and bright blue eyes filled with curiosity and your darling sprouts of hair, I was filled with awe and love for you. I imagined a lifetime of love and closeness when I held you. Never in my wildest dreams could I have imagined that we would end up where we are today, with so much hurt and pain between us.

- Things are clearly not in a good place in our relationship, and that has been the case for quite a while now. You are my precious baby, and I love you so much. I remember like it was yesterday what an amazing, adorable baby you were. When I first held you, you were such a delicious bundle of joy! I could not believe how lucky I was to get to be your mom/dad. You were so bright and lively. Your little personality was shining through, right from the first day! And now, look at where we are, with so much pain and distance keeping us apart.

Considerations

When writing about the length of time of the distance in the relationship, make sure that the phrase you use fits your situation. In the above examples, "a long time" and "quite a while now" were used, but those phrases might not be apt for your specific situation. It might make more sense to say "Recently, it seems that we are not in a good place."

Another consideration for this paragraph is not to add any embarrassing or too intimate details about the birth itself. It would not make sense to discuss the act of birth because most people do not want to contemplate how intimate they once were with their mother's bodies. Likewise, avoid mentioning breast-feeding.

Avoid anything that could be perceived as maudlin or over-wrought. Examples would include mentioning not being happy until the relationship is repaired or extreme sadness at the current situation. Don't open the letter by saying "I am looking out the window as it rains" because that connotes a feeling of dreariness and sadness.

Make sure not to come across as the hero of the story. For example, any mention of the important role you played in saving the day of birth would not be a good idea, even if you were the one who noticed a problem and raced down the hallway to get the doctor, first settled your child when they were a fussy or distraught baby, or fed them the first time. Avoid any effort to put the focus on how important or wonderful you are. That is not in the spirit of the paragraph.

Avoid any superlatives such as "the most amazing baby" or "the best day of my life" if this child has siblings because they might see the letter. Obviously, their feelings could be hurt if they see what you have written. It is possible to convey that over-whelming sense of joy and wonder without using statements that could hurt the feelings of your other children.

A final consideration is to make sure that your description of your baby focuses only on positive details. Mention of how big they were, their crooked toes, or their goofy face would be entirely unhelpful.

Reflections

- *What did it feel like to hold your precious baby for the first time?*
- *What attributes of your baby come to mind?*
- *How are you feeling right now as you think about this paragraph of the letter?*

The Wish for Reparation

Explanation

The second paragraph of the letter is to let your child know that you want to improve the relationship. You recognize that things are not in a great place and feel a strong desire for the situation to improve. You are laying your cards on the table, so to speak, with an honest expression of your heartfelt desire to be closer with your child.

Examples

- You are my precious child, and I want nothing more than to have a better relationship with you, a relationship filled with love and laughter and a sense of safety, happiness, and belonging. I have a vision of our relationship as one filled with love, laughter, and sharing in which you feel and know that I am there for you in the ways in which you need and deserve me to be.

- It feels so wrong for there to be such bad feelings between us. My most heartfelt desire is for us to find a way forward that allows us to have the warm and loving relationship that I want and that I believe you deserve to have. I can imagine a better place for our relationship where you and I share love, laughter, closeness, and caring. I want you to know and feel in your soul that I am there for you in whatever way you need me to be.

Considerations

Make sure to avoid any mention of your pain and suffering or any recrimination of the child (or third party) about how you got to where you are. Any mention of a third party would be very unhelpful at this point, for example, "If [name] had not turned you against me . . ."

Also avoid mentioning anyone else who you believe is suffering from the rupture or difficulties in the relationship such as your family and friends. Bringing in other people who also feel the loss of the relationship could feel unfair to the child, as if you are blaming them for the pain that these other people are feeling. That could cause your child to feel that you are trying to induce guilt, which could result in your child's putting the letter down.

In the example above, the phrase "with love and laughter and a sense of safety, happiness, and belonging" is used. Make sure to reflect on what aspects of your relationship with your child speak to you. You can use the phrase provided if it speaks to your heart. Otherwise, feel free to change it to make it more you.

Reflections

- *What are the essential elements that you want your relationship with your child to embody?*
- *Do you think these elements will also speak to your child's heart?*
- *What can you do to help yourself if you feel flooded with sadness, grief, or other painful emotions?*

OFFER A VISON OF A BETTER FUTURE
Explanation
In the third paragraph of the letter, you are shining a light into the future so that your child can see that there is a way forward to a better relationship with you. Sometimes people assume or feel that the way something is in the present is the only way it can be. Because you are older and have more life experience, you probably know and have experienced firsthand that ruptured or problematic relationships can be healed.

Examples
- One thing I know and believe with all of my heart is that sometimes parents and their adult children have conflict and distance in their relationship and usually they can

find a way to work things out that feels right for everyone. More than anything, that is what I want for us. You may not know this, but [name] and [name] didn't talk to each other for quite a while after a falling out they had. Eventually, they decided to patch things up, and they are both so glad they did.

- I have come to learn over the course of my life that it is possible for relationships to improve and heal, even when they feel so stuck and painful. I don't know if you ever met my friend, [name], but [she/he] and [her/his] [name of her relative] had a lot of hurt and anger in the relationship. Eventually, they found a way to move forward, and [name] says that things are so much better. They still have work to do, but at least, they are both in agreement that this is work they are ready to do. I am feeling hopeful that you and I can come to the same understanding that our relationship is worth working on, and I believe that we have it in us to get to a better place.

Considerations

When writing the story of the two people who had a falling out and worked things out, make sure that it is not a story about you and someone else because that could reinforce the idea that you cannot get along with anyone. Also, avoid making it about the third party who you might feel has contributed to your conflict with your child. That could come across as trying to show the child that this other person is a problem and cannot get along with anyone. Also, refrain from telling a story with details such as "Uncle Joe was upset when Grandpa didn't include him in the will," and make sure that there are no villains or victims in the story such as "Finally, Sally's sister decided to stop being so mean to Sally."

Reflections
- *Do you have personal experience with ruptured relationships being repaired?*
- *Can you set aside your feelings of resentment toward a third party while working on the letter?*
- *Can you access a feeling of hopefulness?*

EXPRESSING INTEREST IN THE CHILD'S POINT OF VIEW
Explanation
In paragraph four of the letter, your intention is to let your child know that you are focusing on their experience of the relationship. This is, hopefully, a novel and enticing idea for your child and will draw them into the letter.

Examples
- I have been thinking a lot about our relationship from your point of view. I am trying to understand what our relationship has felt like for you, what needs of yours were not met, what feelings got hurt, and what aspects of your personhood you felt were unseen by me. I want to understand what this has been like for you so that I can try to make up to you for the ways in which I have hurt you.

- I imagine that I am standing on the banks of a river and you, my child, are on the other side. There is so much that separates us. Rather than trying to explain how things look from my side of the river, I have imagined building a bridge and walking across the river to see how things look from your point of view. I have imagined watching the movie of your childhood, focusing on how things probably seemed and felt to you.

Considerations

The phrase "what aspects of your personhood you felt were unseen by me" can seem awkward. You could try "What aspects of your identity . . ." or "Are there ways in which you feel I have not truly accepted you for who you are?"

Reflections

- *Are there aspects of your child's identity that are hard for you to relate to or that you find off-putting or threatening?*

- *What do you need to do while writing the letter to maintain your focus on your child's perspective, especially when it is inconsistent with yours?*

THREE GRIEVANCE PARAGRAPHS

Explanation

This is the heart of the letter, three paragraphs that address wounds that your child has regarding your relationship. The purpose is to show your child that you can appreciate their perspective and that you are truly willing and able to understand where their hurt is coming from. When trying to determine what grievances to focus on, you can start by looking at homework number 1, the list of what your child might say to someone about why they don't have a relationship with you (see Chapter 11). Try to see if there are big themes that underlie some of the list items. Are there a few items about not being trustworthy, money, being mean to the other parent, violating boundaries, or being angry/moody? See if you can take the list and identify three overarching themes. Each theme then becomes the focus of a paragraph. Each paragraph opens with a statement that you know, think, believe, or understand (depending on how sure you are of this) that the child is upset about this issue. Then tell the story from the child's point of view, how old they were when this happened, and what you think it meant to them. The next element of the paragraph is to ask questions, making sure to demonstrate "compassionate curiosity" with your questions. End the paragraph with a wish about something you could have done differently, bearing in mind that we can always be better in some way or another.

Examples

- I have been wondering if you are still upset about my being the one to end the marriage. You were just a little child, just six years old, when this happened. It must have been so confusing for you to go from living with Mommy and Daddy together in one home to going back and forth between two homes and having Mommy and Daddy not get along so well anymore. What was that like for you to know that I was the parent who chose to end the marriage? Did you feel that if I cared more about you, I would have made a different choice? Were there times when you felt particularly mad at me for making this decision? Were there times when the divorce was particularly hard for you? If I could have done things differently, I would have tried harder to understand what it felt like for you when the family changed, and I would have worked harder to make sure that you felt loved and safe—even though the family was going through such a big change.

- I have also been thinking about your being upset with me because you believe that I stole your college money. This is something that you have shared with me many times over the years. I want you to know that I appreciate your letting me know what was bothering you and I always want to be available to hear your concerns with me. You were in eleventh grade when this was happening in the family. You were focusing on applying to colleges and thinking about next steps in your life journey. It must have been disconcerting to have to wonder on top of everything else about whether there would be enough money for college. What was it like for you to think that I took your money? Did you believe that I demanded to take that money away from you to hurt or spite you? That must have been very confusing for you to think that I would want to take something away from you. I hurt for you knowing that you thought that your mommy/daddy would do that to you. I wish that I had done a better job explaining how the finances were divided after the marriage ended so that you could feel in your heart the truth that I love you and never want to deprive you of what is rightly yours.

- I am also well aware that you are upset with me because I did not agree to buy a horse for you with Daddy/Mommy. That was such a painful time for you when you thought that Billy would be your horse—a dream come true—and then I had to be the one to tell you that it was not going to happen. That must have been a crushing blow for you, to have something almost happen and then have it snatched away. I imagine that you thought about Billy and felt upset with me for a long time afterward. I wonder what you thought about my decision. Did it seem cruel to you? Did it seem to you that I was trying to hurt you and that I was selfish for not agreeing to buy a horse? I wish that I had had the money to buy Billy for you or that I had been comfortable agreeing to buy a horse with your daddy/mommy. I wish that I had been able to convey to you that my decision was not made lightly or out of any ill will for you or your daddy/mommy.

- I know that you are also feeling hurt and angry because you feel that I was often in a bad mood while you were growing up. I do recall times when I was storming around the home, feeling cranky and irritable. I can think of specific times when I slammed a door or banged the kitchen cabinets and you were nearby and probably felt affected by that. You were just a young child at the time, and I can imagine that my irritability created a negative atmosphere in the home that could have been felt deeply by you. How did this affect you? Were there times when you needed me to be available for you and I was too absorbed in my own thoughts and feelings to be there for you in the way that you needed me to be? Did you feel all alone with your feelings? I so wish that I had worked harder to be available to you and not so caught up in my head. I would make sure that you always knew how much you meant to me, no matter what else was going on for me.

• I think another moment in our relationship that has really been weighing on you is when you drove over to my apartment with some important news you wanted to share with me. I recall the moment when I heard the doorbell and could not have imagined that it was you on the other side of the door. I opened the door and saw you standing there, dripping wet from the rain, your eyes filled with trepidation. You had come to share that you felt that you were gay, and I know how much courage that took for you to be ready to share your news with me. It must have been so crushing for you to realize that I had been drinking and was not able to be as receptive and emotionally available to you as you had probably been hoping for. What did it mean to you to see that I had been drinking? Did it feel that I was somehow purposefully making myself unavailable to you? Do you feel that if I really cared, I would have found a way to be more clearheaded in that moment? What was your vision of how I would respond? I want you to know that I fully accept you regardless of whatever identity you connect with. I hope that over the years, I have conveyed that to you, but if not, I am truly sorry for the lapse. I wish I could go back in time and make sure that I did not have anything to drink that evening so that when you came to my door, I would see you standing there in the rain, and I would open my arms to you and let you know through my words and actions how much I love and accept you.

Considerations

These are the hardest paragraphs to write because they require you to set aside your ego, your perspective, and your need to be understood. The moment you add any explanation you have drifted back to your side of the river. An explanation would involve sharing context that makes it seem that what you did was not as bad as the child might think (e.g., I bought you a car and your [other parent] said that they would pay for college). Justification involves blaming the child for the parent's actions such as "If you hadn't . . . then I wouldn't have . . ." Minimization involves trying to convince the child that what you did was not really that bad such as "That only happened that one time, right?"

Note that in the first example, the parent does not remind the child that people don't usually end marriages for no reason, and the parent certainly does not explain what it was about the marriage that led to the decision to end the marriage. In the second example, the parent does not explain exactly what happened with the money, and in the third example, the parent does not explain why she did not buy the horse. The focus is on the child's experience of disappointment. In the fourth paragraph, the parent does not explain why they were in a bad mood, and in the final example, the parent does not explain that they had no way of knowing that the child would make a surprise visit with the intention of sharing some important news. The letter is most effective when the parent refrains from these additions. The main purpose of these paragraphs is to show the child that you are able to see and hold their pain. That is where the healing occurs.

Make sure to use phrases such as "I think that . . ." or "I am wondering if . . ." rather than more definitive statements such as "It must have felt . . ." or "I know that you felt . . ." to acknowledge that you may not fully understand their perspective even though you are trying. You want to leave room for your child to share something new or to add another element to your understanding. Remember that the purpose of this part of the letter is to show your heartfelt effort to put yourself in your child's shoes. It does not require that you know everything 100 percent or that you understand everything fully.

Reflections

- *With whom can you share these paragraphs to get some honest feedback?*

- *What do you need to do while writing the letter to maintain your focus on your child's perspective, especially when it is inconsistent with yours?*

- *Have you addressed the major concerns your child probably has about the relationship, setting aside your ego and perspective?*

THE INVITATION
Explanation

The purpose of this paragraph is to invite your child to share their thoughts and feelings about what you have written. You are letting them know that you are interested in their reaction to the letter and that you want to continue to learn about their perspective.

Example

- You are my precious child, and my heart is filled with love for you. I hope that you can see from this letter that I am trying to understand our relationship from your perspective. I would love to hear your thoughts about what I have written and any other concerns about our relationship that are on your mind. You can respond in writing, on the phone, or in person. We could get together and chat or meet with a therapist of your choosing if you want. Anything that works for you will be fine with me.

Considerations

If your child is highly sensitized to your trying to intrude into their therapy or pushing therapy onto them, it might make sense to remove the mention of seeing a therapist.

Reflections

- *What comes to mind when you think about your child reading your letter?*
- *How does it feel to think that your child will have thoughts and feelings in response to what you have written?*

Sense Memory

Explanation

This paragraph is based on the second component of your homework (see Chapter 11). It is designed to activate the child's positive early attachment feelings with you by your mentioning a positive experience the two of you shared, especially because the experience contained a strong olfactory component.

Examples

- The other day I went to the riverbank by Valley Park and walked around. It looked and felt as magical as ever. I took many deep breaths of that special combination of earth, water, trees, and fresh air that you loved so much. I have so many wonderful memories of taking walks there with you. In the spring, you were excited to see the water rushing by so clear and clean. Do you remember climbing onto the big rock and just sitting there listening to and smelling the waterfall? Those were such lovely times with you. Every time I experience that aroma of clean fresh air and water, I think of you and your joyful love of nature.

- The other day, I was thinking of when we used to make chocolate chip cookies. You were always so helpful and such a delightful baking partner. You loved to help me gather the ingredients, and you were so careful when you measured the sugar, flour, salt, and baking powder. Of course, licking the spoon was a favorite moment for you. Sometimes you got a spot of chocolate on your nose, and you looked as yummy as the cookies. Once they were in the oven, we would usually play a game of cards while the whole kitchen was filled with that lovely aroma of melted butter, sweet brown sugar, and melting chocolate. It was like being inside a warm, sweet cookie. I have so many fond memories of those special times with you and still think of them whenever I smell that delicious combination of warm, sweet, buttery sugar and chocolate.

- I was thinking yesterday about when we used to give Cuddles a bath in the bathtub. It was always exciting for you to help prepare her for the bath and then carry her to the tub. You were so gentle the way you tested the temperature with your elbow, making sure it wasn't too hot or too cold for her. You were like Goldilocks, looking for things to be just right not for yourself but for your beloved puppy Cuddles. I can still smell the yummy aroma of the bubblegum bubble bath, the way the whole bathroom was filled with that sweet, sugary smell. And then when Cuddles would get out and shake the water off, you would be soaking wet but so happy to see your darling Cuddles clean and ready for her next adventure. Animals always brought out your best nature, and I just loved seeing your generous, loving spirit. I still think back to that time whenever I smell that sweet and juicy bubblegum smell, which I just learned is actually a combination of berry, peach, and pineapple. Who knew!

Considerations

Make sure to keep the focus on the child's personality or contribution and stay away from anything that makes it sound like you are the hero of the story, for example, a story of how you helped your child bake one hundred cupcakes, ran to the store to pick up special ingredients, or drove the one hundred miles to go to the perfect beach. Keep the purpose in mind when writing the paragraph. Try to think about what quality of your child's character you want to highlight, such as joyful adventurer; gentle, loving nature; creative spirit; or thoughtful diligence, and then connect that to a specific time and place.

Reflections

- *What does it feel like to summon those sweet memories with your child?*
- *Can you trust that those memories are still within your child as well?*

PHOTOGRAPH

Purpose

The next to last paragraph in the letter focuses on a photograph that you attach of your child when they were about five years old (homework number 3; see Chapter 11). The intent is not to prove to your child that they used to love you, tempting as it would be. The intent is to create a symbolic connection between you and your child, using the picture on the refrigerator as a link. The paragraph starts by mentioning that a picture is enclosed and goes on to tell the story of the circumstances of the picture, with a focus on a positive aspect of the child's character. The paragraph closes by mentioning that the picture is on the refrigerator. Because the

kitchen is the symbolic heart of the home (representing suste-
nance, nurturance, and warmth), the picture is posted there, not
on the desk, mantlepiece, or anywhere else in the home. By plac-
ing the picture on the fridge, your child will hopefully think of you
thinking of them whenever they go into their kitchen.

Examples

- I am enclosing one of my favorite photos of you. You were
  about six years old, and your first baby tooth had just come
  out. You were so adorable! There you are snuggling with
  Fluffy, your pet bunny. You were so careful and loving when
  you held Fluffy, so aware of how she was feeling, so concerned about keeping her warm and safe. Animals always
  brought out your best true self, as I can see when I look at
  this picture of you overflowing with love and joy. I have a
  copy of this picture taped onto my fridge, and every time I
  go into the kitchen, I see your beautiful face and smile.

- Here is one of my most cherished photos of you. You were
  just four and a half when this was taken, and it was one
  of the first times you were at the beach. You can see how
  joyful you were to be in the sun, the sand, and the water
  for the whole day. Your face radiates joy and contentment.
  You begged to be taken back as often as possible, and we
  certainly spent a lot of time at beaches while you were
  younger. And once you learned to swim and dive into the
  waves, there was no stopping you. I think you might have
  been part fish back then! I have a copy of this picture taped
  onto my fridge, and every time I go into the kitchen, I see
  your adorable face and smile.

Considerations

Remember that the photo is not a picture of your child loving
you. The photo should be of just the child. Ideally, they should be
about five years old and should look reasonably adorable (as most

children of that age do) and should not be in a compromising situation (e.g., saggy diaper, naked, or picking their nose).

As noted elsewhere, try to keep the focus on your amazing child and not on you as the hero of the story. Make sure to be realistic. If your child is shown making finger paintings, you don't need to compare them to Picasso. The focus is on their love of painting, not on the masterpieces they made.

If your child has transitioned from one gender to another, try to find a photo in which they don't appear too much of the gender they transitioned away from. For example, if your child was born female and transitioned to male, they may not want to see a photo of themselves in a frilly dress.

Reflections

- *What does it feel like to linger over the picture of your child?*
- *How will it be to have the photo on your refrigerator for you to see every day?*
- *Can you remind yourself that your darling, innocent child is still inside the adult version that you know today?*

The Ending

Purpose

The ending of the letter should be a poetic and dramatic representation of your love and commitment to your child. You want to close the letter with a strong effort to connect with your child's heart.

Examples

- I hope that you can see from this letter that I want nothing more than to repair our relationship and find a way forward so that you can have the mother/father–child relationship that you so richly deserve. My door is open, my arms are open, and my heart is open.

Love,
Your [insert your role here]
- My darling [name]. I love you so much and am committed to doing what I need to do so that you feel ready to have me back in your life. I love you yesterday, today, and tomorrow, from the tip of your nose to the tip of your toes! With much love and hope,
Your [insert your role here]

Considerations

Avoid the statement "I have always been there for you" because it can come across as self-serving and self-important.

Reflections

- *What would be the most impactful way to demonstrate your love for your child?*

- *What kind of closing will touch your child's heart and feel satisfying to you?*

FINALIZING AND SENDING THE LETTER
Getting Feedback

Before you send the letter, you probably want to have another person look at it. You want to make sure that it does not come across as angry, resentful, bitter, self-serving, maudlin, or victimizing. You also want to ensure that you did not leave out a pressing issue, which would come across to your child as avoiding something deeply important to them or as if you are clueless about what is really bothering them.

Timing

Once you have confirmed that the letter is ready to go, the next step is to determine when it should go. Ideally, you will send the letter by email at a time when your child will be away from any influence that could result in their not being able to be open to the letter. If there is a third party that you believe is contributing to your child's disaffection from you, then it would be better if the letter were received when the child is not in proximity to that person. For example, if you believe that the other parent is fostering your child's upset with you and currently your child lives with that parent but is heading off to college shortly, then by all means wait until your child is settled at college and then send the letter.

Sending Methods

It is recommended that you send the letter via email and that you put in the subject line "I am thinking about our relationship from your point of view . . ." Copy the letter in the body of the email as opposed to sending it as an attachment, which the child has to choose to open. Make sure to have three dots at the end of the phrase in the subject header to create an experience of an invitation to read the letter to see what you have to say.

Multiple Children

If you have more than one child who is hurt, angry, rejecting, and distant from you, you probably want to write a letter to each child or send one letter that works for all the children. Do not send a letter to one child and not the others because that could be very painful to the children who do not get the letter. If you are going to modify the letter to fit all the children, you need to change some of the sentences to indicate that the letter is written to more than one child. In addition, the grievance paragraphs have to be expanded to include issues that are relevant to all the children.

Chapter Thirteen

Three Possible Responses

Once you have sent the letter, it is time to sit back and see what happens. You can continue to send text messages if you have already been doing that. Below, we present three scenarios for what happens in response to the letter.

No Response
It is possible that you won't hear back from your child in response to the letter. If this happens, you will not know if they even read it. It probably makes sense to resend the letter one month later just in case they are more receptive the second time around. You can also try sending it to a different email address, sending a hard copy if you have an actual address, or even sending a link to the letter in a text message. There is no harm in resending the letter a few times.

We know how painful it can be to send the letter and not receive any response. You have poured your heart and soul into the letter only to be met with silence. We have certainly heard of situations where the letter was read but not responded to until much later, so try to hold onto the idea that lack of an immediate response does not mean no response ever. In the meantime, we generally recommend that you forge ahead and keep reaching out to your child so they know that you are ready and available when the time is right for them.

Reflections
- *What can you do to prepare yourself for the possibility that you will not receive a response from your child?*

- *Can you imagine your letter as one of many efforts on your part to reconnect with your child as opposed to the one and only message that must succeed?*

NEGATIVE RESPONSE

If your child responds with an angry tirade to your letter, we encourage you to think of this as a good thing because your child does not have to respond to the letter at all. In our view, (almost) any response is a good response because it could be the beginning of a dialogue. The one exception would be a response in which you are told in no uncertain terms to cease and desist all contact. But if the letter from your child contains a critique of your letter and offers ways in which the letter falls short of being adequate, we would consider this very promising—although obviously unpleasant. If you get such a response, we suggest you immediately write back something like "Thank you so much for reading my letter. You have given me a lot to think about, and I will be back in touch after I have reflected more on what you have written." In this way, you are putting out a positive message to your child while not offering an impulsive (and possibly defensive and problematic) response. Perhaps a coaching or therapy session to process your child's letter would be helpful, or using the five steps for false accusations or modified five steps for true accusations (see Chapter 2) would be helpful in formulating a response. Make sure to give yourself the time you need to provide a loving and thoughtful response.

Reflections
- *What can you do to prepare yourself for the possibility of a hurt and angry response?*

- *Can you see the negative response as an invitation from your child for a dialogue?*
- *What do you need to do to refrain from immediately responding to the content of their response?*

POSITIVE RESPONSE

Sometimes the letter results in an immediate positive response from the child, indicating interest in beginning a dialogue with you. That is always wonderful when it happens and what we certainly hope happens for you. We urge you to immediately respond with a message that you are delighted to hear from them that they want to take an initial step forward. The next thing we recommend is that you review Part I of this book to make sure that all of your interactions with your child are designed to convey that you are safe, loving, and available (especially the five steps and the modified five steps). We also recommend that you read (or reread) *Surviving Parental Alienation: A Journey of Hope and Healing* (Baker & Fine, 2014b) because the stories and analyses in that book can help guide you on your path to recovering a relationship with your hurt, angry, rejecting, distant child. It is likely that you will be triggered in your early conversations with your child to feel hurt, angry, rejected, and distant yourself and perhaps resentful and scared of rejection. There are so many feelings that parents in that situation feel; getting a lot of support and guidance can be really helpful.

Reflections

- *How will you maintain your equilibrium if you do receive a positive response?*
- *How can you balance hope and realistic expectations as you take the first step forward?*

RESTORING FAMILY CONNECTIONS

We also recommend that you consider inviting your child to participate in the *Restoring Family Connections* program (Baker et al., 2020) because it was designed to help address the issues that arise when reconnecting with an adult cutoff child. To help you decide if you want to invite your child to participate, you probably first want to look at the activities yourself to see if they appeal to you and seem like the kind of thing that would be helpful. Next, you can try to locate a provider who already knows of the program and/or is familiar with our work so that they would be positively inclined to do the activities with you and your child. The next step is to raise the issue with your child, perhaps saying something like "Now that we are back in touch—and I am so grateful for that—I am wondering what you think of the idea that we do some activities together to make sure that we are working toward the best possible relationship that we can have. It is important to me that you feel safe in our relationship and that we establish trust between us. I have found someone who has some activities that they do with parents and their adult children." It would probably not make sense to mention parental alienation per se or in any way blame a third party or refer to it as therapy. The program is designed to be therapeutic and is implemented by a licensed mental health professional, but it is not therapy per se (i.e., open-ended explorations of thoughts and feelings).

IN CLOSING

We close this book with the sincere hope that you have found the information, suggestions, and ideas helpful, inspiring, and motivating as you work toward the best version of yourself as a parent that you can be. We hope that through your dedication and devotion, your child will be less and less hurt, angry, rejecting, and distant and more and more happy, healthy, loving, and easy to love.

BIBLIOGRAPHY

Adler, A. (1927). *The practice and theory of individual psychology.* Martino Fine Books.

Baker, A. J. L. (2007). *Adult children of parental alienation syndrome: Breaking the ties that bind.* W. W. Norton.

Baker, A. J. L., & Andre, K. (2015). *Getting through my parents' divorce: A workbook for children coping with divorce, parental alienation, and loyalty conflicts.* New Harbinger Publications.

Baker, A. J. L., & Fine, P. (2014a). *Co-parenting with a toxic ex: What to do when your ex-spouse tries to turn the kids against you.* New Harbinger Publications.

Baker, A. J. L., & Fine, P. (2014b). *Surviving parental alienation: A journey of hope and healing.* Rowman & Littlefield.

Baker, A. J. L., Fine, P. R., & LaCheen-Baker, A. (2020). *Restoring family connections: Helping targeted parents and adult alienated children work through conflict, improve communication, and enhance relationships.* Rowman & Littlefield.

Baumrind, D. (1966). Effects of authoritative parental control on child behavior. *Child Development, 37*(4), 887–907.

Chapman, G., & Campbell, R. (2016). *The five love languages of children.* Northfield.

Dreikurs, R. (1991). *Children: The challenge.* Plume.

Gershoff, E. T., Goodman, G. S., Miller-Perrin, C., Holden, G. W., Jackson, Y., & Kazdin, A. (2018). The strength of the evidence against physical punishment of children and its implications for parents, psychologists, and policymakers. *American Psychologist, 73*, 626–38.

Gottman, J. (1998). *Raising an emotionally intelligent child.* Simon & Schuster.

Hart, S. N., Brassard, M. R., Baker, A. J. L., & Chiel, Z. A. (2017). *Psychological maltreatment of children.* In J. B. Klika and J. Conte (eds.), *The APSAC handbook on child maltreatment* (4th ed., pp. 145–62). Sage.

McCloud, C., & Messing, D. (2015). *Have you filled a bucket today?* Bucket Fillers.

Nelson, J. (2006). *Positive discipline.* Ballentine Books.

INDEX